STRATEGIC BOMBING

STRATEGIC BOMBING

JOHN PIMLOTT

GALLERY BOOKS
An imprint of W.H. Smith Publishers Inc.
112 Madison Avenue
New York, New York 10016

Published by Gallery Books
A Division of W H Smith Publishers Inc.
112 Madison Avenue
New York, New York 10016

Produced by
Brompton Books Corp.
15 Sherwood Place
Greenwich, CT 06830

ISBN 0-8317-6027-3

Printed in Hong Kong

10 9 8 7 6 5 4 3 2 1

CONTENTS

THE ORIGIN

At 2205 hours on 13 February 1945, eight de Havilland Mosquito light bombers of the Royal Air Force (RAF) began to unload red target markers over the German city of Dresden. Ten minutes later, the first of 244 Avro Lancaster heavy bombers dropped its high explosives. Over the next 15 minutes, a mixture of high explosive and incendiary bombs laid waste to the center of the ancient city.

But Dresden's agony was not yet over. More bombers arrived three hours later. Between 0130 and 0150 on 14 February, a further 529 aircraft added to the burning mass. One crew reported a 'fantastic glow from 200 miles away,' another that 'from 20,000ft Dresden was a city with every street on fire.' A total of 773 RAF bombers dropped 2978 tons (including 650,000 incendiary devices) during the two-phased attack, which lasted in all for a mere 35 minutes.

The effect was truly devastating, for a firestorm had been created – the ultimate holocaust of what was known as strategic bombing. As the large central fire burned, it heated the atmosphere above, which in turn sucked in cooler air from surrounding areas to cause a tornado effect. This rushing wind fanned other flames, so that temperatures rose to an estimated 1000°C as the many different fires joined together. Dresden became a vast burning sea, while high-explosive bombs mixed with the incendiaries prevented fire services from tackling the blazing wasteland. The number of people who died is not known for sure, but some historians think it may have been as high as 135,000.

What happened in Dresden was no accident. For 30 years commentators had predicted that a mass force of bombers would obliterate a city. Before the outbreak of World War II in 1939, it was even argued than an entire country could be driven to surrender by a 'knock-out' blow from the air against its capital – the sort of paralyzing blow experienced by the citizens of Dresden. This had not, in fact, been far from the minds of those who planned the Dresden raid: Operation Thunderclap, which looked for a dramatic demonstration of airpower to persuade the German government that continued resistance was futile, had been discussed at a high level. The firestorm of 13/14 February 1945 was an attempt to achieve that aim. As such, it represented the theory of strategic bombing at its most extreme: not simply damage to one city, but the surrender of a whole nation.

To discover how these extravagant hopes had built up, it is necessary to look back to World War I (1914-18). Between 1915 and 1918, bomb-dropping German airships killed 528 and injured 1156 civilians in England; two short aeroplane raids on London in June and July 1917 together led to 896 casualties. They had a lasting effect upon the people at large, as well as politicians and military planners.

Ten years before the raids on London, as enthusiastic pioneers risked (and frequently lost) their lives in unstable aeroplanes – flimsy concoctions of wood and canvas, powered by primitive, smelly engines – or hung precariously beneath the volatile, gas-filled envelopes of airships, such destruction seemed mere fantasy.

Writers like H G Wells did imagine a mass airship attack on cities like New York causing 'civil conflict and passionate disorder,' but most servicemen dismissed aeroplanes as 'interesting scientific toys, of little or no practical value for the purposes of war' or as 'a useless and expensive fad.' Most countries developed airships or aeroplanes for nothing more than reconnaissance and observation, and even then there were those who doubted the value of such machines, arguing that it was impossible to see clearly what was on the ground while flying over it at 30mph.

Thus it was that in August 1914, when war broke out in Europe, airpower seemed to have a very limited potential. In Britain's case, for example, a few biplanes, lacking range, speed and firepower, wobbled across the Channel to France to carry out 'armed reconnaissance,' but were incapable of doing anything more, least of all long-range bombing. The Royal Flying Corps (RFC), as part of the British Army, and the Royal Naval Air Service (RNAS), as part of the Royal Navy, were distinct organizations, together mustering 272 aeroplanes, of which only 90 were serviceable. Britain and her allies together only had 1235 machines, plus eight airships, and the situation was little different among their enemies. Germany, Austria-Hungary and Turkey (who joined the so-called Central Powers later in 1914) deployed 1410 aeroplanes and 19 airships. Of the latter, 15 were German, constructed either of aluminum (Zeppelins) or wooden (Schütte-Lanz) frames. The United States of America, neutral until 1917, had about 350 aeroplanes,

PAGES 6-7: The crew of an Armstrong Whitworth Whitley bomber walk toward their machine prior to an air-test, 1940.

LEFT: American bombs, delivered by B-17 Flying Fortresses of the Eighth USAAF, rain down on Dresden, 14 February 1945. The city is still burning from the previous night's 'firestorm.'

ABOVE RIGHT: Searchlights bracket a Zeppelin airship over London, 1915. Even with such illumination, the airships were extremely difficult to shoot down.

RIGHT: The city of Dresden, photographed in March 1946, more than a year after the 'firestorm.' Levels of destruction are high, although a few public services have been restored.

all of 'inferior types.' It was not an impressive picture.

The Germans were the first to undertake what would become known as strategic bombing – the deliberate by-passing of the land battlefield to attack an enemy's cities and factories, so going for his heart rather than his frontline muscle. Early in 1915 German airships bombed East Anglia and shortly afterward London from their bases across the North Sea, aiming quite deliberately to unnerve the capital's population and undermine the national government. For the theory that air raids would destroy not just buildings but also the morale of the civilian population was beginning to gather force. Already, the Germans had established an aeroplane unit (disguised as a Carrier Pigeon Unit) of 36 Aviatik B-Type machines at Ostend to hit England, although failure to capture the Channel ports in France and southern Belgium in 1914 meant that they lacked the range to reach their targets. Nevertheless, the intent was clear.

To a certain extent, this was satisfied by the airships, which flew at 60mph and could discharge ballast to climb at 1200 feet a minute to reach 23,000 feet – well above the maximum altitude of antiaircraft guns and defending aircraft. Moreover, they certainly did have the range. Airships could bomb accurately, being able to stop or slow down over a target, which was impossible for an aircraft. Navigation, though, was not always easy. Depending on dead reckoning and radio cross-bearings, the airship could be frustrated by cloud, winds and rain, while defensive successes did occur. However, they were rare: during 1916, only five out of 111 airships attacking England were shot down.

In truth, some raids on London were quite effective. In September 1916, for example, a single airship caused £500,000 of damage in one night. The colorful destruction of a Schütte-Lanz raider over Cuffley that month, when crowds watched it crash spectacularly in flames,

ABOVE LEFT: The crew of a Zeppelin airship.

LEFT: The remains of Zeppelin *L.32*, brought down by a fighter near Billericay in Essex, September 1916.

BELOW LEFT: Once the fires have gone out, only the gaunt skeleton remains: Zeppelin *L.33*, September 1916.

ABOVE: The sleek lines of German Naval Airship *L.53*.

RIGHT: A searchlight mounted on the Old Lambeth Bridge, London.

could not disguise the impact of the airship raids. They continued until August 1918, even though improved fighter aircraft and a better organized antiaircraft barrage reduced their overall impact during the later months. In November 1914 Admiral Tirpitz had undoubtedly exaggerated when he claimed that 'the English are now in terror of Zeppelins,' but the civilian population was clearly unsettled and vital war work in factories disrupted by air-raid alerts. What is more, toward the close of 1916, airship raids were tying down 110 interceptor aircraft, numerous guns and searchlights, plus 17,341 officers and men that could have been used instead to boost the frontline across the Channel.

In 1917, Noel Pemberton Billing MP declared: 'We know what a disturbing effect air raids have in this country and how cheaply the effect is gained.' By then, the aeroplane (which added to the airship menace in the spring of that year) had become a major problem. The increased range of aeroplanes meant that England could now be hit by Gotha G-IV and later G-V machines from German-held territory in Belgium. Capture of the Channel ports was no longer necessary. Initial raids on southeastern England included one on Folkestone on 25 May that killed 95 and injured 195. A furore broke out as the 'appalling sight . . . (of) dead and injured persons lying on the ground . . . the wholesale murder of women and children' grabbed the headlines. To make matters worse, 74 defending aircraft failed to account for a single attacker.

More raids on the southeast were followed by the two distressing attacks on London. On 13 June 17 Gothas killed 160 people in the capital, injured 408 and caused £130,000 of damage. Fifty-two defending aircraft achieved nothing, while 'spent' antiaircraft shells, falling back to earth, caused a further 20 casualties. Calls for 500 aircraft to 'pay back the enemy in the same way as he has treated this country' and 'ceaseless air attacks on German towns and cities,' found vocal support, particularly in the popular press. But the British lacked sufficient aircraft to launch such a campaign, nor in fact did their planes have the range to reach German cities, even from bases in France.

Another daylight raid on London on 7 July reinforced the mixture of panic and anger at shortcomings in the current defenses. This time, 53 people were killed and 190 injured, with antiaircraft fire causing a further 65 casualties from spent shells. Public pressure demanded that fighter aircraft be withdrawn from the frontline in France to protect the capital.

During the winter of 1917-18, the Germans switched to night bombing, reinforcing the Gothas with larger *Riesen* or R-Type bombers, appropriately known as 'Giants.' On 6 December 1917, six Gothas did £92,477 of

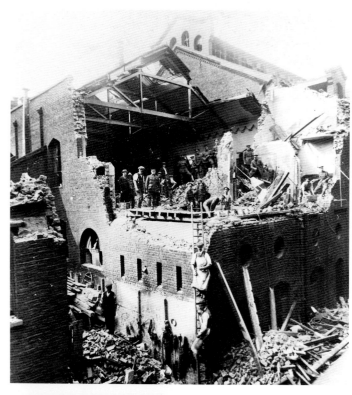

ABOVE: Servicemen and workers review damage to King's Cross station after a Gotha raid, 17 July 1917.

LEFT: Damage inflicted on a workhouse laundry in Islington, 5 September 1917.

ABOVE RIGHT: A balloon 'apron,' erected to cover the approaches to London, 1917. The idea was to force the bombers to fly high, so reducing their accuracy.

LEFT: A Gotha bomber stands ready to carry out an attack, its bomb-load attached to special racks beneath wings and fuselage.

RIGHT: An RFC officer discusses the finer points of his Bristol F2B fighter with Queen Mary, while Lord Trenchard looks on.

damage and, for the first time, ominously dropped incendiary bombs. A raid by three Gothas and one Giant on 28 January 1918 produced another chilling statistic: £173,000 of damage to property, 51 people killed and 136 injured through enemy action. Even more dramatically, 38 of those killed and 85 of the injured all came from one incident, when a bomb undermined the foundations of Odhams Printing Works in Long Acre, sending the heavy printing presses crashing down on to the cellars being used as shelters. Panic in other shelters, caused when warning maroons were mistaken for German bombs, added a further 28 to the casualty list. One Gotha was shot down, but the War Office quite understandably expressed concern at the destructive power of the large bombs (up to one ton) now being used by the enemy. Loss of sleep, interruption to manufacturing production and a more general effect on people's nerves were now seen as a direct consequence of the bombing raids.

Rather like the Germans, the British gradually and, to some extent, casually drifted into strategic bombing, as the range and bomb-carrying capacity of aircraft increased. The need to destroy German airship sheds was an initial spur to aircraft development, and all-purpose machines soon gave way to specialist fighter, bomber and reconnaissance designs. In 1914 Winston Churchill (then First Lord of the Admiralty) viewed a 30-mile flight over enemy territory as 'a very serious business' of only limited effect − the biggest bombs available were only 20lbs. Two years later, 330lb bombs had been specially designed for long-range bombing and, before the end of the war, 1650lb bombs were in production.

During 1915 Major-General Hugh Trenchard, then in command of the RFC in France, formed 'special squadrons' to carry out 'sustained attacks' on 'German strategic centers' beyond the trenches. A year later he was advocating a 'relentless and incessant offensive' on 'places of importance behind the lines.' At this stage, Trenchard had in mind strictly military targets like ammunition dumps and railway centers connected with bringing supplies of men and materiel to the trenches, although significantly he held that 'the moral effect produced by hostile aircraft is out of all proportion to the damage which it can inflict.' That belief would remain with him throughout his life.

Meanwhile the RNAS had used its shore-based aircraft to attack the Zeppelin sheds, and early in 1916 was looking toward attacking steel plants at Essen and Düsseldorf. Industrial rather than strictly military targets were now on the bombing agenda. In the winter months of 1916-17, an RNAS Wing concentrated at Luxeuil and, in cooperation with French squadrons, bombed an impressive array of targets: the smallarms factory at Oberndorf, iron works at Hagendingen, and armament factories in Volkingen, St Ingbert and Dillingen. In addition to direct damage, the Germans were obliged to withdraw aircraft, searchlights, balloons and antiaircraft guns from the frontline to defend sensitive industrial areas − just as the British had been forced to do to protect London.

The idea of 'long-distance bombing machines operating against blast furnaces and munition factories' in German territory was widely acclaimed in Britain and 'their excellent effect both materially and morally' applauded. But pressure to provide close cover to troops in the trenches, given the overall lack of available aircraft

LEFT: A Handley Page 0/100 bomber, fitted with four 200hp Hispano-Suiza engines, mounted in tandem. This is an experimental machine: the 0/100 normally had only two engines.

BELOW LEFT: A Handley Page V/1500 four-engined heavy bomber, designed to bring Berlin within range of airfields in East Anglia. The war ended before any such raids could be carried out.

RIGHT: Jan Christian Smuts (seated, left) at the 1923 Imperial Conference in London. Six years earlier, his reports on aerial bombardment had put forward extravagant claims for strategic bombing.

at the front, meant that the Luxeuil Wing had to be disbanded. Nevertheless, by 1917 both the RFC and RNAS had independently carried out long-range bombing raids on enemy territory. The British War Cabinet now accepted that 'a long-range offensive is in itself a most desirable thing' and ministers variously argued that 'the offensive is the only radical cure' (for enemy raids on England) and 'an aggressive retaliatory policy is of the first importance.'

In this climate of opinion – dread of enemy raids and belief that British bombers could effectively damage Germany – the South African politician Jan Christian Smuts produced two reports in August 1917 for the British War Cabinet on the future of airpower. The second of these advanced extreme claims for the bomber (the first dealt with air defense), and provided one persuasive argument for setting up a separate air force completely independent of the other two services (the army and navy). Strategic bombing would be its main role, taking the bombing to the enemy in retaliation for the raids on England.

Smuts believed that, such was its potential, the Air Service should be seen 'as an independent means of war operations.' He went on: 'The day may not be far off when aerial operations with their devastation of enemy lands and destruction of industrial and populous centers on a vast scale may become the principal operations of war, to which the older forms of military and naval operations may become secondary and subordinate.' Powerful stuff and bound to upset the other two services.

It was clear from Smuts' evidence that he had been very much affected by the German raids on London, which he had personally experienced. Referring to the trench struggle on the continent, he held that while the armies edged forward at a snail's pace, 'the air battle front will be far behind on the Rhine and . . . its continuous and intense pressure against the chief industrial centers of the enemy, as well as on his lines of communication, may form an important factor in bringing about peace.' The centerpiece of Smuts' second report was a recommendation that a separate air force (in addition to the army and navy) be formed.

While the debate about whether or not the Royal Air Force should be created continued at home (it was resolved on 1 April 1918 when the RAF officially came into existence), British bombers were apparently supporting Smuts' arguments in action. In October 1917, another British bombing unit was formed in eastern France within reach of Coblenz, Mannheim and Cologne, the coal and iron fields of Lorraine and industrial centers of Luxembourg. This force was expanded in 1918 'to attack, with as large a force as is available, the big industrial centers of the Rhine and in its vicinity.' In five months the Independent Bombing Force, commanded by Trenchard , dropped 500 tons of high explosive on to German targets, so that the British Secretary of State for Air became 'strongly convinced of the effectiveness of long-range bombing on German civilian morale and on limitation of industrial effort.'

During the closing weeks of the war, No 27 Group RAF concentrated in Norfolk, equipped with the new four-engined Handley Page V1500 – the first purpose-built

strategic bomber, capable of reaching Berlin from England. It did not fly in anger before the Armistice in November 1918, but it stood as a monument to the belief that large, long-range bombers could make a distinct contribution to warfare. In view of its later commitment to strategic bombing, it is significant that during 1918 the United States launched a bombing offensive from bases in France against industrial targets in the Metz area. American crews raided 15 German cities, claiming 1303 casualties.

By November 1918, therefore, the theory of strategic bombing had been widely accepted and, to some extent, put into practice. The early German attacks on England had pointed to raids on towns being potential morale breakers. As technological advances created larger aircraft with greater range and increased bomb-carrying capacity, the choice of targets widened. French officers believed not only that bombing of enemy towns had created 'a state bordering on panic,' but that attacks on 'munition centers' (and more especially steel works) had also been successful.

What emerged from World War I was the confidence that a bombing campaign directed at enemy cities and factories would undermine enemy morale and fatally affect his capacity to wage war. That was the essence of strategic bombing. Unfortunately, it was little short of unproven faith. Overall, morale did not break to the extent that any nation's determination to fight evaporated, not were the claims of widespread industrial damage from the air borne out once the relevant evidence had been examined postwar. The Handley Page V1500, though, remained a tangible demonstration of blind faith, and its image would very much be a potent force in strategic and military thinking in the years to come. Perhaps the most influential statement to emerge from the immediate postwar inquest was that of Trenchard: 'The moral effect of bombing stands undoubtedly to the material effect in a proportion of 20 to 1.'

Once the war was over, in Britain the very future of the RAF was called into question. Both the army and navy argued vehemently that it should be broken up, with the other two services regaining air arms and control over their use. In other words, the RFC and RNAS should be recreated. Trenchard, then Chief of the Air Staff and the RAF's most senior officer, had to defend his service against increasingly bitter attacks. He set out to prove that the new third service would make a peculiar contribution to war. To demonstrate effective support of the army in the trenches or the navy at sea would not do. Strategic bombing – an independent means of winning wars, if Smuts' more extreme claims were accepted – provided Trenchard with his strongest defense. Added to this was evidence of overseas achievements in the postwar years.

Afghanistan had for long been a troublesome area to the northwest of British India. There were genuine fears that, as she expanded her empire, Russia would seek to dominate the weak Afghan government before moving eastward against India. In 1919, yet another conflict between the Afghans and British was in progress, with no solution in sight. Seizing the opportunity to demonstrate that bombers could win wars, Trenchard sent a Handley Page V1500 to bomb Kabul, the capital of Afghanistan, in May. The effect was dramatic. Within days the Afghans had sued for peace: the 'big bird' had caused panic among the people, who had never seen an aircraft (let alone a bomber) before. A few bombs had quite literally won the war, saving in the process the expense of a military expedition. That same year rebel tribesmen in Somaliland (East Africa), led by the 'Mad Mullah,' were similarly put to flight by a squadron of bombers flown specially from Egypt. In three weeks, they achieved more than ground troops had in years. Afghanistan and Somaliland greatly enhanced the credibility of an independent RAF.

Seizing on the British government's search for economy in military spending once peace had been signed in Europe, Trenchard persuaded ministers that aircraft could 'police' colonial territories more effectively and more cheaply than the army. In 1922, bombers quelled a revolt in Iraq, and the RAF soon assumed formal responsibility for controlling the whole of that area. Its methods were to bomb villages suspected of harboring rebels, and they worked – at least for some years. The evidence of successful 'imperial policing' operations not only helped to keep the RAF independent,

LEFT: A Vickers Vimy heavy bomber. Like the V/1500, it was designed to carry out attacks on Germany that never took place. It continued in RAF service until 1931.

RIGHT: Brigadier-General 'Billy' Mitchell poses next to a VE.7 aircraft at the Bolling Field Air Tournament, May 1920.

BELOW RIGHT: An American aircraft hits the battleship hulk USS *Alabama* with a phosphorus bomb during trials held at Mitchell's suggestion in September 1921.

by showing that it could act independently, but it also reinforced the growing belief in bombing (and, by implication, in strategic bombing) as a major contribution to war.

Trenchard was no paper theorist. He used practical experience, carefully presented, to argue that bombing must be the mainstay of the British aerial war effort. The best means of defense, he argued, was attack. If the RAF could pose a clear threat to any potential enemy, by training a bomber force capable of smashing his cities and factories at the outbreak of war, that enemy would think twice about quarreling with Britain. The threat of a strategic bombing campaign, much more terrible than anything delivered by the German airships or Allied biplanes of World War I, would deter another country from action. If, however, it was rash enough to fight, RAF bombers would destroy Berlin or Paris as they had Kabul in 1919, not by mass devastation but by creating public panic. Pursuing this line of argument, Trenchard shaped the composition of the RAF between the two world wars. In so doing, he also effectively defended the independence of his service.

In 1923, bombers made up two-thirds of the RAF's Home Defence Force. The British homeland, Trenchard explained, was best protected by showing a hostile neighbor that Britain was capable of a massed bomber strike against him. This claim did not appear unrealistic, as giant strides began to take place in aeronautical engineering – larger engine capacity and load-carrying capability, retractable undercarriages, closed cockpits, metal rather than fabric fuselages, monoplanes in place of biplanes. As long-distance, intercontinental flights became commonplace and aircraft bigger, the idea of heavy bombers with decisive bomb-loads no longer seemed fantastic. Strategic bombing became the declared faith of the RAF and it seemed natural therefore that a Cabinet Minister, Stanley Baldwin, should exclaim in 1932: 'the bomber will always get through.' Three years later, he was more specific. Massive air attacks would produce 'tens of thousands of mangled people – men, women and children.'

In the United States, airpower had no independence: unlike in Britain there was no separate air force. William

('Billy') Mitchell, a serving officer who had commanded American flying units during World War I, became a vigorous advocate not only of airpower but of an independent US Air Force. He faced arguments that bombers were offensive weapons, whereas American declared policy was one of defense. The navy could best defend the coastline; aircraft should merely support the other two services. Using anchored battleship hulks, Mitchell showed that capital ships were vulnerable to bombing and in two books, *Our Air Force: The Keystone of National Defense* and *Winged Victory*, he aggressively expounded his ideas, using data from his experiments. Higher authorities were not amused. When Mitchell, in deep frustration, accused the Department of Defense of 'incompetency, criminal negligence and almost treasonable administration of National Defense,' he did not escape court-martial. But he used his trial – in which he was found guilty – to reach a wider audience. In 1930, he repeated his opinion, which was very similar to that of Smuts and Trenchard: 'The advent of airpower, which can go straight to the vital centers and entirely neutralize or destroy them, has put a completely new complexion on the older system of war.'

Then, in 1934, 10 twin-engined B-10 bombers flew nonstop from Alaska to Seattle, and supporters of strategic bombing thus had a weapon. Soon, too, the four-engined machine became a reality and, in 1937, Brigadier-General Frank M Andrews wrote: 'I am convinced that the four-motored bombing plane is the weapon of hope for this nation.' Like Mitchell, he suffered for his candor, although later he was to serve with distinction in World War II.

Mitchell and Andrews were faced with a persistent, active naval lobby. Admiral William D Leahy declared that 'battleships are the best modern defense weapons' and, during the Spanish Civil War (1936-39), Admiral Clark H Woodward said: 'Airships (aircraft) can never win a war; they can never win a battle.' Undeniably, bombing enthusiasts were relying mainly on theory; sailors had a string of impressive victories to quote.

However, aircraft designers were now developing much more impressive bombers. Following the success of the Martin B-10, an all-metal monoplane capable of 200mph and a ceiling of 28,000 feet, came the Boeing B-17 and Consolidated B-24 four-engined aircraft. Both used the liquid-oxygen system developed in 1928 to allow airmen to operate at high altitude and the Norden bombsight, which claimed pinpoint accuracy. Carrying multiple machine guns for their own defense and bomb-loads of some 5000lbs, the Flying Fortress and Liberator (as these aircraft became known respectively) would make an invaluable contribution to Allied bombing campaigns during World War II. In 1939, though, the US still lacked an independent air force. Mitchell's fierce support of

strategic bombing theory may not have paid off in this respect, but undoubtedly the US now had the potential to carry it into practice. Moreover, the idea of a bomber with adequate means for its own defense in the air had been born.

Test flights of the B-17 commenced in 1935 and the first B-24 flew in 1939. In 1936, the RAF set out specifications for four-engined bombers, though it would take another five years before the first of these types went into service. Despite Trenchard's work and belief that bombers would be decisive in a forthcoming conflict, in 1939 the RAF went to war with nine different types of bomber. None was four-engined and only two-thirds were capable of reaching the industrial heartland of Germany (the Ruhr) from England. This, in itself, was an indictment of forward planning. In 1937, the British Air Staff had drawn up elaborate plans to deal with Germany in the event of war, which by then seemed inevitable. The mainstay of those plans was an aerial assault on German factories in the Ruhr – the centerpiece of strategic bombing theory, hitting the enemy's industrial capacity to wage war. Curiously, too, the Germans had been slow to develop heavy bombers. General Walther Wever, their staunchest advocate, was killed in an air crash in 1936 and thereafter enthusiasm waned. Hitler saw armies as the nub of his military machine and demanded aircraft to support them. Experience of the German Condor Legion in Spain also gave the misleading impression that twin-engined bombers were effective. The awesome destruction of the Basque town of Guernica in 1937 underlined this conclusion.

In Italy, another strong supporter of the bomber had gone into print. So impressive were his arguments that,

BELOW LEFT: A Vickers Wellesley general-purpose bomber in 1938 camouflage. The Wellesley was the first RAF aircraft to employ geodetic construction.

RIGHT: The remains of the Basque town of Guernica, bombed by the German Condor Legion in 1937 during the Spanish Civil War. Its destruction became a powerful symbol of the impact of bombing.

RIGHT: A Heinkel He-111B of the Condor Legion drops its bombs over Valencia during the Spanish Civil War. The conflict was used as a proving-ground for German techniques of bombing.

although as with Mitchell, he initially offended his superior officers and was court-martialed, Giulio Douhet has become closely associated with the concept of strategic bombing, to the extent that the very idea is sometimes simply called 'Douhetism.' Like Trenchard, Douhet recognized the need to avoid another long war, wasteful in men and money. The mass bomber raid, launched against enemy cities, would cause disintegration of civilian morale. Industrial centers were equally vulnerable to such attack. It was necessary, Douhet claimed, 'to hammer the nation itself to make it give in.' In his book, *Command of the Air*, not fully translated into English until 1942 but freely discussed long before that, Douhet in effect set out yet again the basic tenets of strategic bombing. There is some evidence that military officers in France and Germany were aware of Douhet's views, but in reality those views were not unique: Trenchard and Mitchell showed that. However, he did forecast the use of gas bombs, in much the same way that artillery had used gas shells during World War I, and although this too had been widely canvassed in Britain, it helped to create the need for elaborate precautions. By 1939 every man, woman and child in Britain, for example, had been issued with a personal gas mask.

By 1939, therefore, strategic bombing had grown rather than diminished as a perceived means of waging war. Moreover, it had been refined into the most dangerous concept of a 'knock-out' blow delivered by massed bombers in daylight at the outset of any new war. In 1938 an official estimate expected 3500 tons of bombs to fall on London in the first 24 hours of a war, with 700 tons a day to follow. A 500-plane raid (considered the most likely) would kill 20,000 people and the opening 24 hours would account for a total of 100,000 in London alone. Thoroughly alarmed, as the political situation deteriorated rapidly, the British Government increased its expenditure on Air Raid Precautions fivefold to a staggering £51 million in 1938-39. No wonder that, brainwashed by warnings of devastating air attack, thousands of Londoners rushed into air-raid shelters minutes after the Prime Minister, Neville Chamberlain, broadcast the news that the country was at war with Germany on 3 September 1939.

The air-raid warning proved to be a false one, but the theory of strategic bombing had had its effect. People dreaded enemy bombing attacks as eagerly as staff officers planned them. It was all a long way from those tiny biplanes that staggered over the Channel in August 1914 to support the soldiers. The fires of Dresden in February 1945 had metaphorically already been lit.

TESTING
THE THEORY

Once more, as with their initial airship raids on England, the Germans were first to carry out a strategic bombing campaign when hostilities recommenced in 1939. Waves of bombers struck Warsaw in September to hasten Polish surrender and, in May 1940, Rotterdam felt the weight of Luftwaffe power before the Netherlands capitulated. These strikes were not sustained affairs, although it could be argued that the Warsaw raids over such a short period of time, in effect, constituted the aerial 'knock out' blow so feared in England. That fear was manifested in a variety of ways. Apart from the issue of gas masks to the entire population, the digging of air-raid shelters, the provision of 2.8 million hospital beds to cope with expected casualties and of 20 million square feet of seasoned timber each month for coffins, the British Government evacuated 1.5 million women and children from centers of potential danger like London, Liverpool and Southampton. Many other families fled to 'the country' unassisted by official agencies.

Yet during the 'Phony War' (September 1939-May 1940), nothing happened in Britain. By the time that the German raiders did arrive in force, in the latter half of 1940, many evacuees had drifted back home and a renewed exodus to comparative rural safety away from burning buildings and high-explosive destruction occurred. Curiously, too, for all the prewar planning, neither the French nor the British attempted to hit Germany — and, in particular, its vulnerable Ruhr industries — before Hitler invaded France and the Low Countries on 10 May 1940, despite having been at war by then for eight months. So much for preemptive strikes, knock-out blows and undermining the enemy's capacity to wage war. What might have been the eventual outcome if Allied bombers from continental bases had attacked the Ruhr while Germany fought Poland?

It was left to Reichmarshall Hermann Goering's airmen to test the theory of strategic bombing against Britain, once France had surrendered in June 1940. For its aerial assault, the Luftwaffe had air fleets in France, the Low Countries and Norway. Together they had some

PAGES 20-21: An aerial shot of Rotterdam, hit by German bombers on 14 May 1940. Exaggerated rumors of the death toll from this raid did much to increase public fears of bombing in Britain.

ABOVE: Reichmarshall Hermann Goering, head of the Luftwaffe, visits his aircrews during their attacks on Britain, 1940. He was convinced that the Luftwaffe could drive the RAF from the skies.

LEFT: Dornier Do-17s fly in daylight formation against targets in southern England, summer 1940. They were ineffective strategic bombers.

ABOVE: Luftwaffe groundcrew manhandle a 500kg bomb toward a waiting Heinkel He-111, about to take part in a raid against England, 1940.

RIGHT: A Messerschmitt Bf-110 twin-engined escort fighter, 1940. Known as the *Zerstörer* (Destroyer), the 110 proved no match for the single-engined interceptors of the RAF.

RIGHT: A Heinkel He-111 bomber of *Kampfgeschwader* (Bomber Group) 26 is prepared for action, 1940.

3300 aircraft (approximately one-third Messerschmitt Bf-109 and Bf-110 fighters, the rest single-engined Junkers Ju-87 Stuka dive-bombers, and Heinkel He-111, Junkers Ju-88 and Dornier Do-17 twin-engined medium bombers). The British defenses, which aimed to prove that, contrary to prewar belief, the bomber would not always get through, consisted of 700 fighters (single-engined Supermarine Spitfires, Hawker Hurricanes and Boulton-Paul Defiants, plus a few twin-engined Bristol Blenheims) organized into four Groups to cover the southwest, southeast, Midlands and north; antiaircraft guns and barrage balloons around important installations such as dockyards and large cities; Observer Corps posts with listening devices and visual identification equipment mostly in the coastal areas; and a thin chain of just 12 Radio Direction Finder (RDF, known as radar) aircraft detection stations along the shores of East Anglia and the southeast. Air Chief Marshal Sir Hugh Dowding, Air Officer Commanding-in-Chief, RAF Fighter Command, coordinated the system of aerial defense through a command structure that reached downward from his headquarters through Groups and stations to squadrons, which scrambled aircraft to engage the incoming enemy.

LEFT: Part of the British Chain Home radar system, vital in giving early warning of German attacks in 1940. The masts are designed to give the radar extra range.

RIGHT: Dornier Do-17s fly over the Thames toward West Ham during the daylight raid on 7 September 1940 – the beginning of the 'Blitz' on London.

LEFT: A British Observer Corps post during the winter of 1940. As one mans scans the skies for German aircraft, another stays in radio contact with his headquarters.

BELOW: A Dornier Do-17P, with a Junkers Ju-88 in the background. Both types flew in the attacks on England in 1940-41.

Hitler ordered Goering 'to overcome the British air force,' so that its command of the air over the English Channel would be removed. Operation Sea Lion, the German invasion of Britain, would then be launched. The date for that was set, rather optimistically, at 15 September. During June and July, the preliminary phase of what became known as the Battle of Britain took place, with determined German attacks on shipping in the Channel and on south-coast ports like Southampton, Weymouth and Portsmouth. The attackers did not escape lightly: between 10 July and 10 August, they lost 217 planes. However, despite the fact that many of its pilots, baling out over friendly territory, were saved, the RAF suffered 96 losses, and factories were hard pressed to make up the deficiencies, let alone to increase Fighter Command's total number of available aircraft. On one day, for example, No 54 Squadron had only eight planes for 13 pilots.

'Eagle Day,' when the massed German air fleets would concentrate to destroy the RAF, was fixed for 11 August. Bad weather forced a postponement for two days, then on the 13th the Luftwaffe mounted 1485 sorties, suffering only 45 losses. The Germans convinced themselves that 30 airfields and, more crucially, 30 factories had been eliminated that day. Yet very soon, the falseness of this optimism became only too evident. Fighter Command was still active and hopes that hundreds of its aircraft had been destroyed began to fade.

In fact, German ability to hurt the RAF was limited by the range and defensive capability of its bombers.

ABOVE: A barrage balloon is brought to earth. Launched over vulnerable targets and tethered to the ground, these balloons were designed to prevent low-level attacks by aircraft.

RIGHT: Bomb damage near the Old Bailey, London. Despite a considerable battering by the Luftwaffe bombers, London did not cease to function.

Failure to develop a four-engined machine meant that only the southern part of England could be effectively attacked; attempts to bomb from Norway farther north proved of limited value. Moreover, the lightly armed and comparatively slow twin-engined Heinkels and Dorniers were easy prey to the faster and more maneuverable Spitfires and Hurricanes. As a result, they had to be protected by Luftwaffe fighters, which could never decide whether to do so in close support or by more far-reaching sweeps. Furthermore, there was a distinct absence of planning on the German side. In their daylight raids of August and September, their bombers were directed at too many different targets – the radar chain (which Goering soon abandoned as too difficult to locate and hit), fighter airfields, bomber airfields, factories and, to some extent, towns. This confusion of targeting can only be explained by the arrogant and unrealistic presumption that, despite heavy casualties among the bombers at the beginning of a campaign, they would triumph through the cumulative effect of destructive power.

LEFT: A Heinkel He-111 flies over Wapping during a daylight raid on London, 7 September 1940. The photograph was taken at 1848 hours.

RIGHT: As fire hoses play on the front of the building, the roof burns brightly – bomb damage in Pimlico, April 1941.

BELOW: Londoners shelter in the Underground, 1940. In this case, the normal trackway (on the left) has been converted to a sleeping area.

BELOW RIGHT: On the night of 11/12 January 1941, a German bomb penetrated the Bank Underground station, caving it in and killing 55 people. The crater, shown here, was enormous.

Between 24 August and 6 September the Luftwaffe mounted 33 major raids. Success proved elusive, and Sea Lion was postponed to 27 September. On Sunday 15 September, Goering sent 427 bomber and 708 fighter sorties against London. It was the gambler's last throw: he lost 60 aircraft on that one day alone. The attempt to devastate London in a single knock-out blow by day had failed; more crucially, in the context of the war as a whole, Sea Lion was canceled. The Germans, like Allied planners in their attacks on Germany during World War I, now recognized that bombers were vulnerable to fighters by day. They therefore switched to night bombing against British cities. Pinpoint accuracy at night was difficult to achieve, though: individual factories could not always be hit, so towns and cities in general became targets. Attacks on civilian morale were, after all, an integral part of strategic bombing theory.

London, in particular, suffered. Between 7 September and 2 November 1940, the capital was raided for 57 consecutive nights. Whole streets were destroyed, transport and other public services disrupted and people made homeless. During that relatively short period, 13,561 tons of bombs were dropped, and to escape their effect, Londoners took refuge in basements, Anderson shelters dug in back gardens and even Underground station platforms. Then the enemy bombers widened their 'Blitz,' as the campaign was popularly known in Britain. Provincial centers did not escape: on 14 November, 449 bombers attacked Coventry, dropping 503 tons of high explosive and 881 canisters of incendiaries; 554 people were killed, 865 seriously injured and 21 major factories were damaged. On 10 January 1941, 171 people were killed and 430 injured in Portsmouth; Liverpool, Manchester and Hull were among many other towns to suffer as the enemy employed radio beams and special path-

finder squadrons to guide their bombers to their targets.

The last major raid of the winter hit Birmingham on 16 May 1941. By then, though, it was obvious that the Luftwaffe's attempt to cow the population, undermine morale and adversely affect manufacturing production had failed, despite the fact that 30,000 civilians had been killed and 3.5 million made homeless. Factories in Coventry were back in action five days after the November 1940 raid, and in Portsmouth the chalked sign on a public house, which boasted cardboard in place of shattered windows, summed up the local spirit: 'Blasted out but not sold out.' Efficiency of civil defense services – foreseen with the prewar accent on Air Raid Precaution spending – was one reason for public resilience. In the air, fighters were beginning to acquire their own radar equipment, and on the ground searchlights and anti-aircraft batteries were becoming more effective. By spring 1941, the dark skies were no longer quite as safe for attacking bombers. Yet still, belief in the ability of bombers to hit the morale of civilian populations and to destroy the enemy's fighting capacity by destroying his factories persisted. Prime Minister Winston Churchill wrote: 'There is one thing that will bring Hitler down, and that is an absolutely devastating, exterminating attack by very heavy bombers from this country upon the Nazi homeland.' Unfortunately, the experience of the Luftwaffe over England (and of early RAF raids over Germany), had already suggested that such a decisive campaign was little more than a pipe dream.

In 1939, in spite of belated emphasis on the production of fighters which allowed Dowding scope to win the Battle of Britain, the RAF still placed its faith firmly in a bombing offensive. Discounting the single-engined Fairey Battle light bombers and other obsolescent types, Bomber Command had 17 squadrons of 'powerful' twin-engined Armstrong-Whitworth Whitleys, Vickers Wellingtons and Handley Page Hampdens when the war began. Officially, they would 'leap across the protective barrier of his (the enemy's) armies and strike him at vital centers, so as to destroy his factories and oil refineries, and to disrupt his communications – in a word, to dislocate and bring to ruin his military economy.' Smuts, Mitchell, Douhet and Trenchard would most certainly have approved. For this was the very kernel of strategic bombing theory. Lacking the four-engined self-defending bombers being developed in the United States, all this was to be achieved in daylight with the twin-engined bombers flying in formation to provide a measure of mutual protection.

This tactic was put to the test shortly after the war began. With targets on German soil forbidden and explicit orders issued to avoid any possibility of civilian casualties (for fear of provoking a powerful reaction), British squadrons instead concentrated on German naval units in the Heligoland Bight. Its strong, distinctly unfriendly defenses soon earned the nickname 'Hornets' Nest' from the bomber crews. Admissions of 'fairly severe

ABOVE LEFT: A Handley Page Hampden of No 16 OTU: the slender fuselage and twin engines made the aircraft a poor strategic bomber.

LEFT: Vickers Wellington I bombers of No 9 Squadron, RAF Bomber Command, photographed early in the war. The ribs of the Wellington's distinctive geodetic construction may be clearly seen.

ABOVE: The crew of an Armstrong Whitworth Whitley bomber look on as the groundcrew prepare the aircraft for action. The yellow symbols depict raids already carried out.

RIGHT: Short Stirling four-engined bombers fly over the flat lands of Lincolnshire, 1941.

casualties' were not effectively countered by hopeful (and, in fact, misleading) statements that 'crews of the Wellingtons were very well satisfied with the mutual fire power developed by the power-operated turrets' or that enemy fighters had been deterred from attacking formations of Wellingtons and Hampdens. The casualty figures told another story. Faster, more maneuverable Messerschmitt Bf-109 and Bf-110 fighters quite simply 'hacked down' the British, in the words of one bemused airman: '0.303in machine guns were no match for 20mm cannon.' The loss of 12 out of 22 Wellingtons on a raid against naval targets in Schillig Roads on 18 December 1939, with the enemy pursuing homebound survivors well into the North Sea, proved the death knell for the RAF's hopes that bombers could successfully and decisively press their attacks. The Air Ministry now admitted that 'we should have to accept heavy casualties if we attacked in daylight.' More pointedly, Pilot Officer G P Gibson (later to achieve fame as commander on the Dambusters Raid) observed: 'It was hell for the crews and uneconomical for the country.'

Not only were the bomber crews experiencing the uncomfortable, often fatal attention of aggressive fighters, but antiaircraft batteries also proved unpleasant as the twin-engined aircraft failed to climb out of range. Attempts at dismissive humor – 'the natives appear too hostile' – could not disguise this lethal danger. The vagaries of meteorology had also to be faced. 'Violent changes in the speed and force of air currents, fog and the formation of ice on an aircraft in flight are formidable adversaries,' one navigator recorded. He might have added that electrical storms threatened fire and were also prone to interfere with the accuracy of instruments like the compass. All in all, it was a nasty environment.

RAF losses in daylight, like those of the Luftwaffe between July and September 1940, pointed the way to night bombing, as did the success of leaflet raids by Whitleys which ranged deep into Germany with scant interference. At length, the night of 11/12 May 1940 saw bombs fall on the German mainland, when 18 Whitleys attacked railroad targets near München-Gladbach. It was, the Air Ministry acknowledged, a 'modest and unassuming' beginning to the strategic bombing campaign against Germany. Four days later, 93 'heavy bombers' flew against oil plants and blast furnaces at Duisburg and the Air Ministry could enthuse that, for the first time in this war, 'the hot glow of fires and the jagged flashes of exploding bombs colored the darkness which shrouded the chief industrial area of Germany.' That was more like it: attacks spread to other targets in the Ruhr and even farther afield to Bremen and Hamburg. Between 29 May and 5 June 1940, 350 bomber sorties took place. Sadly, they achieved little. Another official communique disclosed that 'the German war machine was not seriously affected.'

This disappointing scenario did not improve. The fall of France in June 1940 meant that bombers lost their continental bases, so putting many completely out of reach of the Ruhr. Moreover, fear of invasion determined that priority had to be given to dealing with barges that were being gathered across the Channel ready to carry out Operation Sea Lion. The force available to bomb German industrial targets was, therefore, much reduced. 'By the beginning of July,' one officer wrote, 'the bomber crews were just about all in.' 'Heavy damage,' 'consider-

able damage' or 'much devastation' were claimed for attacks on cities from Berlin to Mannheim, and production from oil plants at Gelsenkirchen was also, apparently, greatly reduced. During an attack on Emden on 1 April 1941, 'masses of debris flying through the air were outlined against the glow of fires.' By June 1941, 1666 attacks of more than six aircraft had taken place on German territory; Gelsenkirchen had been raided 28 times between 27 May and 2 December 1940. Brave attacks were carried out, too, on specific targets like the viaduct of the Dortmund-Ems Canal, and the Hamm marshaling yards were visited over 80 times between June 1940 and June 1941.

Despite claims of 'serious damage' to such industrial centers, photographs of gutted tenement buildings in Berlin and Aachen revealed that cities in general, rather than individual factories, were now being bombed. Not that this strayed from one of the basic tenets of strategic bombing theory – the undermining of civilian morale. Flying by night to evade the enemy defenses may have reduced bomber losses (at least initially), but it did nothing for accuracy. By spring 1941, the official bombing error at night was 300 yards, but privately planners suspected 1000 yards to be a truer figure – always provided that the bomber could actually reach and identify the target.

As early as December 1940, stark evidence emerged that attacks were not being carried out as accurately as crews reported. Two key oil plants were situated at Gelsenkirchen. Bomber Command believed that one had been attacked by 162 aircraft carrying 159 tons of high explosive, the other by 134 aircraft with 103 tons. A considerable number of incendiaries had also been dropped. Yet daylight reconnaissance photographs on 2 December showed that the production capacity of neither had been affected: both were still working.

LEFT: A battery of German 88mm guns occupies a rather exposed position, 1940. These guns were capable of putting up a formidable anti-aircraft barrage.

RIGHT: Josef Kammhuber, shown here (center) as a major-general commanding a night-fighter group, was responsible for creating the highly effective 'Kammhuber Line' of anti-air defenses in Europe.

Realization that pinpoint accuracy could not be attained led to a gradual assumption that an average error of 1000 yards, not 300, was indeed more realistic. As a result, transport areas, like marshaling yards, replaced oil plants as preferred targets. But even these could only be attacked with any confidence on moonlit nights, which tended to negate the advantages of switching from daylight bombing in the first place. On 9 July 1941, the Air Staff went further, pointing out that 'for approximately three-quarters of every month it is only possible to obtain satisfactory results by the 'Blitz' attack on large working class and industrial areas of the towns.' Bomber Command was directed toward 'dislocating the German transportation system and to destroying the morale of the civilian population as a whole, and of the industrial workers in particular.' Dwelling houses in Berlin, Aachen and other German cities were due to be revisited time and again by RAF bombers. What became known as 'area bombing' had been sanctioned.

A report by a civil servant, David Butt, in August 1941 reinforced the suspicion that crews were not achieving the accuracy they claimed. Making use of 650 photographs taken by bombers either at the aiming point or at another specified position in the target area during 100 separate raids on 24 targets over 48 nights, in conjunction with other relevant data like plotting reports and operational summaries, Butt reached some unpalatable conclusions. Of those aircraft reported to have attacked their targets, only one in three had got within five miles. This figure included France and Germany; for Germany alone, the figure was one in four. The chilling additional fact was that for the Ruhr (the centerpiece of prewar strategic bombing plans), that fell to a mere one in 10. These statistics related to aircraft claiming to have attacked the target; taking into account sorties that admittedly went astray, overall only one in five of the

bombers got to within five miles – or 75 square miles – of their targets. Thick haze, a new rather than a full moon and intense antiaircraft fire made the figures even less attractive. In those circumstances, the figure for the Ruhr dropped from one in 10 to one in 15. It was all reminiscent of the World War I pilot who reported, somewhat colorfully but honestly, 'theoretically it was a beautiful shot, practically it hit a turnip.'

Undoubtedly, the bombers lacked adequate navigational aids, and bomb-sights were not entirely satisfactory. But improvements in the German defenses played a very important part in defeating the bombers' intentions. The lessons of the German failure over England were being painfully relearnt by the RAF. In the early months of the campaign, the Germans relied mainly on antiaircraft (flak) fire to keep bombers high so that they would not bomb accurately. The more faint-hearted might even be persuaded to off-load their cargoes away from the target. Day fighters – types that had devastated the early British formations over Heligoland Bight – were sent up hoping by 'pure luck' to glimpse and engage an enemy bomber.

Then, in autumn 1940, Major-General Josef Kammhuber, the Luftwaffe's Chief of Night-Fighters, began to deploy a belt of searchlights (through which incoming bombers would have to fly) to illuminate the bombers for interceptor fighters; he also sent aircraft on intruder operations over British airfields to catch bombers as they took off or landed in the glare of revealing flight-paths. This rather crude system was gradually improved, especially when airborne radar became available for twin-engined fighters, which then began to specialize in the night-fighting role. By the middle of 1941, Kammhuber had further improved his defensive system. On the coast *Freya* radar sets with a range of 100 miles provided early warning of bombers approaching across the North Sea. Two shorter-range *Würzburg* sets operated on the ground, one locking on to a bomber and the other guiding the fighter into range, whereupon it could use its onboard radar set to complete the interception. Aircraft and radars were positioned in a series of interlocking zones (or 'boxes') which came under the direction of divisional control rooms for coordination of the regional defensive effort. One drawback was that only one fighter could be controlled in any zone at a given time. Kammhuber also developed special night-fighter squadrons which by the close of 1941 were starting to score significant successes.

The British organization of attacks played into the hands of the German defenses at first, as aircraft were encouraged to fly separately to the targets and to spread their attacks over a lengthy period of time to cause maximum disruption (it was argued) to enemy civil defense services. How and when different aircraft attacked was up to the crews. Squadrons were given a time-span at briefing during which they had to attack; in extreme cases, this was hours rather than minutes. Such was the latitude offered that crews were known to visit the cinema or local inn for refreshment before setting out. Routes were the responsibility of captains and navigators, and precisely how aircraft attacked once over the target was up to the crews. Some pilots chose to glide to the target instead of flying at speed over it. In theory, these piecemeal attacks would confuse the ill-organized German defenses: very wishful thinking, as it turned out. So, for a variety of reasons, the bombing offensive was not going at all well by the end of 1941. In November, only an average of 506 bombers were available, many of them obsolescent twin-engined types. A staggering 37 were lost on the night of 7/8 November, forcing Bomber Command to reduce its effort for some time.

Publicly, the Air Ministry put on a brave face: 'The proportion of bombers that reach their destination, always very high, is growing higher. The target is hit again and again.' Pointing to the introduction of four-engined bombers such as the Short Stirling and Handley Page Halifax into service, it further promised: 'These aircraft are to deliver that overwhelming onslaught which will bring the enemy to his knees and then lay him prostrate in the dust of his own ruined cities. No chosen target can escape them.'

Brave words, indeed, but yet again blind faith was needed to accept that this time the bombers would really get through. Having done so, they would find their actual (not imagined) targets and then bomb them accurately. In truth, the evidence so far was not encouraging: Kammhuber's defenses were quite obviously getting stronger and more effective.

At the beginning of 1942, therefore, the fortunes of RAF Bomber Command were very much at a low ebb. The strategic bombing campaign had clearly not succeeded. Far from achieving a knock-out blow, after nearly two years of effort, the German war machine seemed quite unaffected. Meanwhile, U-boats were threatening to starve Britain into early submission. Bombers might, it was argued, be better employed patrolling the sea lanes. As a result, the very survival of Bomber Command, let alone the future of the strategic bombing campaign against Germany, was very much at risk. There was more than the occasional whisper in high places that perhaps it ought to be disbanded.

ABOVE LEFT: A German *Würzburg* radar set, photographed in Russia in 1942.

ABOVE: A Short Stirling of No 218 (Gold Coast) Squadron, RAF Bomber Command, receives its load of incendiaries prior to an attack on Wilhelmshaven.

LEFT: A German *Freya* radar set, situated near Brest in northwestern France, 1942. Incoming aircraft could be picked up at reasonably long range using this equipment.

RIGHT: A Handley Page Halifax Mark I awaits squadron delivery, 1942. The arrival of the Halifax gave the RAF a new strategic capability.

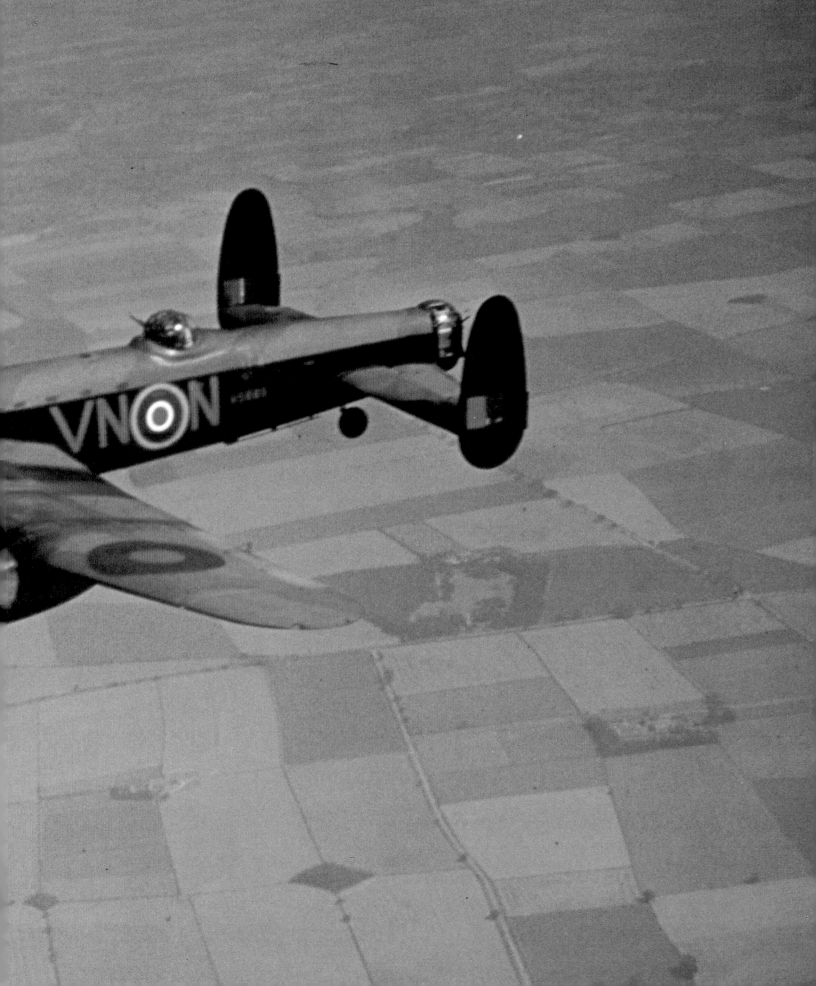

REFINING
THE WEAPON

It was obviously time for positive action. Abandoning the last pretence of precision bombing against selected targets, on 14 February 1942 the Air Staff went even further than its directive of 9 July 1941. Bomber Command was told quite categorically that 'the aiming points are to be the built-up areas not, for instance, the dockyards or aircraft factories.'

Eight days later, Air Marshal Arthur Harris took charge of Bomber Command. His orders were, therefore, to mount an area-bombing campaign against Germany. He was promised improved means of doing this. In March, the four-engined Avro Lancaster (a development of the unsatisfactory twin-engined Manchester) came fully into service and a new navigational aid – the *Gee* radio beam equipment – reached 15 operational squadrons. However, with enemy advances in North Africa and the Far East, coupled with mounting naval pressure for long-range bomber support in the Atlantic, Harris' more immediate task was to ensure the survival of his command. He had to demonstrate that Germany could be bombed effectively.

After three disappointing raids against Essen earlier in the month, on 28 March 1942 Harris sent 234 bombers to the Baltic port of Lübeck. Using *Gee* for navigational accuracy, leading aircraft illuminated the medieval town with flares and incendiaries. More than 200 acres and 2000 buildings were destroyed in the subsequent attack, causing Josef Goebbels, the Nazi Minister of Propaganda, to complain that 'no German city has ever been attacked so severely from the air.' The raid occurred in bright moonlight, Lübeck was easily identifiable because of the coastline, had weak defenses and consisted largely of wooden buildings that burnt well. Nevertheless, the operation was undeniably spectacular, and Winston Churchill enthused to President Franklin D Roosevelt: 'Our new method of finding targets is yielding most remarkable results.' *Gee*, though, was only a

navigational aid and visual identification of the target remained necessary – a difficult task even in ideal meteorological conditions if faced by strong defenses. Even so, at the end of March, Lord Cherwell, Churchill's chief scientific adviser, estimated that attacks on 58 large German towns would break enemy morale by mid-1943.

Shortly afterward, during four successive nights (23-27 April 1942), a total of 847 tons of incendiaries and high explosives fell on Rostock: 70 percent of the city was flattened and 100,000 people made homeless. Hitler appeared 'in extremely bad humor'; Goebbels thought the damage 'catastrophic,' with 'community life there practically at an end.' The RAF lost just 12 planes. Then, on 30/31 May, 1046 bombers attacked Cologne in a single night – a deployment that Harris, in a deliberate ploy to grab public attention and support, could only achieve by using his entire frontline force and a substantial part of his reserve. Over a period of 90 minutes,

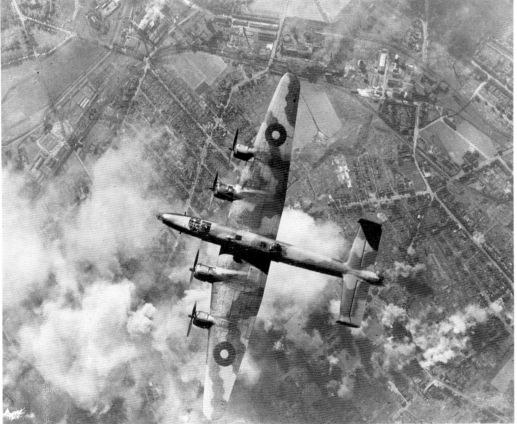

PAGES 36-37: An Avro Lancaster of No 50 Squadron, photographed in August 1942.

ABOVE: Air Chief Marshal Sir Arthur Harris (center, in glasses), plans a night raid against Germany, 1943.

ABOVE RIGHT: An aerial photograph shows part of the destruction caused in Cologne during the first of the RAF's '1000-Bomber' raids, 30-31 May 1942.

ABOVE, FAR RIGHT: Luftwaffe men check the radar equipment on a Messerschmitt Bf-110.

LEFT: A Handley Page Halifax Mark III, photographed over a synthetic oil plant at Eikel in the Ruhr, late in the war.

the center of Cologne was transformed into 'rubble and ruins': 460 people were killed, 45,000 made homeless, and over 3000 houses and 36 factories were utterly destroyed. It cost Bomber Command 41 aircraft. This devastating assault was followed by further 'Thousand Bomber' raids on Essen and Bremen in June, although with less spectacular results. These three efforts, together with other operations like that on Lübeck, took the pressure off Bomber Command; perhaps, it was said, strategic bombing would work after all.

The organization of Bomber Command's night operations had by now vastly improved. Gone were the days of casual, individual attacks. The bombers were now concentrated into streams which set out deliberately to swamp Kammhuber's 'box' system. One enemy fighter per box could scarcely cope with hundreds of attackers. However, the Germans were not slow to react. Their night-fighters became more self reliant as better airborne detection aids were fitted to them. Searchlights and antiaircraft guns were grouped around vulnerable targets, ready to put up dangerous 'box barrages.' Such was the strength of the defenses of the Ruhr, that crews ironically dubbed the area 'Happy Valley.'

Although Harris undoubtedly did step up the bomber campaign, one unpalatable fact was apparent. Although in February 1942 about one percent of aircraft on a typical raid were falling victim to night-fighters, by October that figure had risen to more than five percent. Allowing for deaths through wounds and other causes, an individual member of a Bomber Command aircrew had scarcely a 10 percent chance of completing his allotted tour of 30 operations. A staggering total of 50 bombers failed to return from Bremen on 26 June.

Several developments did hold out hope of improvement. In August 1942 a special Pathfinder Force (renamed No 8 Group in January 1943) was formed, with the task of leading main-force aircraft to their targets and marking them accurately. Pathfinders released yellow flares at designated turning points along the route, then red flares to mark the approach run and finally green ones at the aiming point. Sky markers, too, were introduced, so that in bad visibility crews could bomb onto these without requiring ground identification. In January 1943, more sophisticated Target Indicator Bombs were brought in – 250lb light-case weapons that burst 3000 feet above the ground to cascade onto the targets thousands of small red balls which burned for five minutes. The colors could be varied to prevent German decoys.

During the autumn of 1942, however, the Germans began to jam *Gee*, which thereafter had only reduced value. In December, though, *Oboe* came into service – an improved radio beam device capable of being used by a few aircraft to pinpoint the target. It was ideal for the

Pathfinders and especially for the new high-flying de Havilland Mosquitoes – the 'Wooden Wonders' that were now the mainstay of Pathfinder operations. H_2S, an airborne radar carried in the bombers themselves, appeared in January 1943. This produced a ground image and was particularly valuable in distinguishing land from water. But its emissions could be detected by alert night-fighters. *Oboe*, H_2S and sky markers greatly assisted bombing accuracy; so did the 'all-singing, all-talking, all-dancing' Mark XIV bomb-sight. As one pilot remarked: 'Old man weather, the last obstacle of all, had been overcome.' A shade optimistic, as events were to prove.

In March 1943, with this new range of bombing aids fully operational, the Battle of the Ruhr began. Having 660 heavy and 300 medium (twin-engined Wellington) bombers at his disposal, Harris held out 'real hope of success in the task which had been given to me when I first took over the Command at the beginning of 1942 – the task of destroying the main cities of the Ruhr.' During the night of 5/6 March, *Oboe*-equipped Mosquitoes, backed up by other Pathfinder bombers, led a main force of over 400 aircraft to Essen. In 38 minutes, 1054 tons of bombs were dropped, laying waste to 160 acres and making 30,000 people homeless. In four other attacks during the course of the 'battle,' 1552 aircraft dropped 3967 tons onto Essen. Goebbels was furious about the 'inadequate defenses.'

In fact, while the Battle of the Ruhr lasted from March to July 1943, some 2700 sorties were flown against Essen, though Düsseldorf, Dortmund, Bochum and Duisburg also suffered heavily. To keep the Germans from concentrating fighters in the Ruhr, cities like Berlin, Stettin, Pilsen, Munich and Stuttgart were raided as well. In all, 18,506 sorties were flown in 43 major attacks. The cost was not low: excluding 2126 aircraft damaged or lost on their return to England, 872 bombers (containing around 6000 airmen) were shot down over Germany. While the Battle of the Ruhr was in progress, No 617 Squadron carried out its celebrated night-precision attack on west German dams on 16/17 May. But the prolonged period of training required for this operation, and the high loss rate (50 percent of the attacking aircraft failed to return), in reality showed that such accuracy was beyond main-force squadrons.

Toward the end of July, Hamburg was singled out for a savage assault. Four night attacks between 24 July and 2 August were carried out by bombers equipped with the improved Mark II *Gee* and H_2S, preceded by the Pathfinders. For the first time, bundles of metallized strips designed to confuse enemy radar sets – known as 'Window' – were dropped. Eighty flak, 22 searchlight and some three smokescreen batteries were rendered impotent, their *Würzburg* radars blinded. Night-fighter airborne radar was also affected. In all, over 9000 tons of bombs (approximately half of them incendiaries) were dropped in 3095 sorties, for the loss of 86 bombers. More significantly, the second of the raids created the first deliberate 'firestorm,' an elaboration of which would gut Dresden in February 1945. In association with two American daylight attacks, the RAF assault on Hamburg killed 41,800 people, injured 37,439 and damaged 277,330 buildings. Over a million survivors fled the city. Goebbels declared the attacks 'a real catastrophe' and Albert Speer, the Minister for Armaments and War Production, believed that similar attacks on six other important cities would finish the Reich. The RAF certainly tried. Between July and November 1943, its four-engined bombers flew 17,021 sorties in 33 major raids on German cities, losing 695 aircraft with another 1123 damaged.

Harris then argued for one of the long-standing beliefs

FAR LEFT: The crew of an Avro Manchester wait to board their aircraft, 1942. The Manchester, underpowered and difficult to fly, was not popular.

LEFT: A Consolidated B-24 Liberator and its crew, 1942. The B-24, developed as a four-engined heavy bomber, was designed to survive in daylight, but losses were soon to mount in the skies over Germany.

ABOVE: Boeing B-17 Flying Fortresses of the 381st Bombardment Group, Eighth USAAF, fly over the English countryside, 1943.

RIGHT: The remains of a chemical plant in Germany hit by the Eighth USAAF. Chemical and oil targets were a priority for the American bombers.

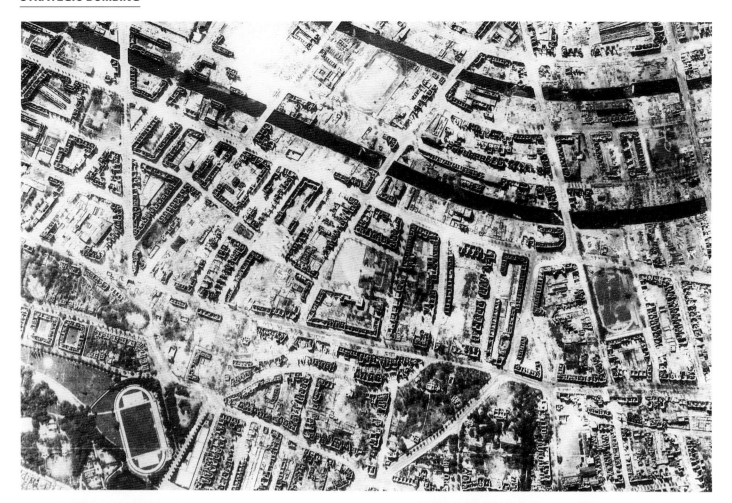

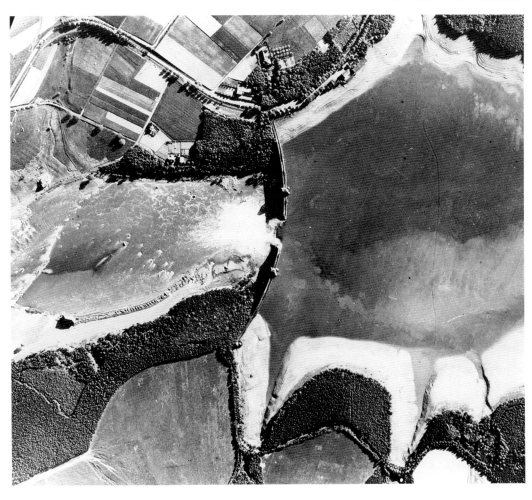

LEFT: The remains of part of Hamburg, hit by the terrifying ordeal of a 'firestorm' in late July 1943. Whole areas are completely burnt out.

RIGHT: The Möhne Dam, hit by Lancasters of No 617 Squadron on the night of 16/17 May 1943. Although spectacular, the attack did less permanent damage than originally hoped for.

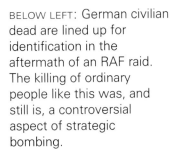

BELOW LEFT: German civilian dead are lined up for identification in the aftermath of an RAF raid. The killing of ordinary people like this was, and still is, a controversial aspect of strategic bombing.

of strategic bombing theorists: that destruction of an enemy's capital would cause political collapse. With more powerful means at his disposal than the Luftwaffe which attacked London in 1940-41, he foresaw success. He told Winston Churchill that, if the Americans joined with Bomber Command, 'we can wreck Berlin from end to end.' This would cost, he reckoned, 'between us 400-500 aircraft, it would cost Germany the war.' The Americans disagreed. So, on 18 November 1943, Bomber Command alone launched the first of 16 major raids on Berlin, the last being on 24 March 1944. Quite apart from the Pathfinders, 9112 bomber sorties were flown, 29,341 tons of bombs were dropped. Over four square miles of the German capital were devastated, 1.5 million people made homeless. In the initial six raids alone, 46 factories were destroyed and 259 damaged. Goebbels noted: 'Hell itself seems to have broken over us.'

As with the Battle of the Ruhr, attacks were also made on other cities to distract the defenses. In all, including the raids on Berlin itself, 20,224 sorties were flown. Despite variation in tactics and the various new aids available, 1047 bombers were lost and 1682 damaged. The final operation in the so-called Battle of Berlin was against Nuremberg on 30/31 March 1944. It proved an unmitigated disaster. Of 795 attacking aircraft, 95 failed to return, 12 more were lost after crossing the English coast on the way back, and another 59 were severely damaged. The loss rate was almost 12 percent. Bomber Command could simply not afford such carnage. Without command of the air, the bombing campaign was doomed.

This is precisely what the Americans, once they became involved over Europe, set out to achieve. The self-defending bomber would deal with any airborne threat from fighters and, having fought its way successfully to the target would, using precision bombing from high altitude during daylight, demolish armament and in particular aircraft factories. The experience of the Luftwaffe and RAF in 1940-41 was invalid: they had lacked bombers of the caliber of the Flying Fortress and the Liberator.

The first B-17 Flying Fortress of the US Eighth Army Air Force (AAF) touched down in England in July 1942. By the close of the year, approximately 300 Fortresses and B-24 Liberators had arrived. Their crews were not overjoyed with the climate: 'English mud is infinite in its variety and ranges from watery slop to gelatinous mess with all the properties of quick-setting cement' was how one flyer put it.

Twelve B-17s made the initial all-American raid over the continent, hitting marshaling yards at Rouen in occupied France on 17 August 1942. This and subsequent missions were carried out unscathed; the first B-17 was not lost until 6 September. In October, B-24s went into combat and, to provide mutual defensive fire, Colonel Curtis LeMay developed an elaborate combat 'box' system for the task forces that made up the vast armadas of US bombers. Between 17 August and 31 December 1942, American heavy bombers flew 1547 sorties for a loss rate of only two percent. The omens for attacking Germany were therefore good, even though, as yet, only occupied countries had been hit. But, truth to tell, for these short-range missions the 'self-defending' aircraft were actually escorted by fighters.

Then, on 27 January 1943, 53 B-17s and B-24s hit Wilhelmshaven. Three aircraft were lost, and the problem of accurately assessing the numbers of enemy fighters apparently destroyed by air gunners was starkly revealed.

The more extravagant claims were whittled down to an acceptable 22, yet in reality the Germans lost just seven. In February, 22 American bombers were shot down and losses began to creep up: 16, with another 44 damaged, out of 115 attacking Bremen in April; 22 out of 60 against Kiel in June; and, during 'Blitz Week' in July, over 100 lost or scrapped. By the end of July, there were fewer than 300 American heavy bombers still operational in England. The vulnerability of the heavy bomber in daylight had been cruelly exposed. But the Americans resisted pressure from Harris to change to night bombing. They argued that it would take too long to retrain crews. Quite obviously, though, the bombers could not fly without proper fighter escort, and one crucial drawback was that, with short-range capability, the fighters could only reach the German border in the area of Aachen from England and no more. Thereafter, the bombers had to fight their own way to and from the target. LeMay's combat boxes helped them, but they still suffered grievous loss.

Two raids on the ball-bearing factories at Schweinfurt in Bavaria underlined this. In theory, destruction of Schweinfurt's factories would literally bring the German war effort to a grinding halt. The Norden bomb-sight, it was argued, would create the accurate bombing needed to achieve this. From Aachen to Schweinfurt and back was a 400-mile, unescorted flight. Throughout this the bombers would be mercilessly harassed by formations of enemy fighters, while at the target, the five factories were ringed with formidable flak defenses.

The first raid took place on 17 August 1943 — attractively, the first anniversary of the American operation against Rouen. This time, the story would be different. In an effort to confuse the enemy, one task force was to

ABOVE: A B-17, its wing severed by cannon fire from a German fighter, spirals earthward. American daylight losses were high in 1943, calling the whole campaign into question.

ABOVE RIGHT: Avro Lancaster I R5868 'S-Sugar,' on the completion of its 100th operational sortie.

LEFT: Bombs explode around the ball-bearing factories at Schweinfurt, Bavaria, 17 August 1943.

RIGHT CENTER: A North American P-51D Mustang fighter. When this aircraft became available in late 1943, it could escort the daylight bombers to Berlin.

BELOW RIGHT: A Republic P-47 Thunderbolt fighter, affectionately known as the 'Jug.'

attack the Regensburg aircraft factories, 120 miles southeast of Schweinfurt, then fly on to North Africa, as two other task forces hit Schweinfurt itself. Bad weather disrupted these well-laid plans, and the Regensburg force went ahead separately, before the Schweinfurt planes were airborne. The Germans were therefore able to concentrate on the Regensburg bombers first, with dire results. But the Schweinfurt raiders came off even worse. Once the protective Spitfires and Republic P-47 Thunderbolts had turned back, a furious air battle raged. Of the 196 B-17s to attack Schweinfurt, 36 were lost (only one of them to flak, the rest to fighters); the Regensburg force lost 24. Thus, in one day, 60 aircraft (containing 600 men) went down. The Regensburg force lost a further three aircraft on the way back to England and left 60 more badly damaged in North Africa. Together, the two attacking forces claimed over 200 enemy aircraft destroyed: in fact, the Germans lost 25. Disappointingly, too, the 'severe damage' allegedly caused to the factories at Schweinfurt in reality only partially interrupted production for a maximum of four weeks.

The belief remained, though, that Schweinfurt had to be 'practically destroyed or, at the very least, seriously crippled' to strike a decisive blow at the enemy. On 14 October 1943, therefore, the Eighth AAF went back. Once more, elaborate plans were laid. This time, two B-17 task forces and one B-24 task force would converge on Schweinfurt alone. Lockheed P-38 Lightnings with special drop-tanks of fuel to improve their operational range would sweep ahead of the bombers. Such was the

luck of the crews heading for the target, that the Lightnings were not available on the day. Moreover, between 8 and 10 October the Americans lost a massive 88 aircraft, with another eight written off. So for Schweinfurt, in the end, only 324 B-17s could be mustered to tackle the 900-mile trip, half of it unescorted. Bad weather caused cancellation of the B-24 task force, so the Fortresses, flying in two task forces slightly apart, were left to fight their way through alone. Due to poor visibility over England, fighters did not meet them as arranged on the return journey, so enemy aerial attacks continued beyond Aachen into the Low Countries. Of 260 bombers which ultimately pressed their attack, only 195 landed safely and a mere 63 of these were relatively undamaged. German fighters accounted for 58, flak for two and five more crashed after crossing the English coast. The second Schweinfurt raid was the fourth costly mission in six days.

Like the Germans and British earlier, the Americans now acknowledged the severe problems involved in mounting daylight attacks, especially deep-penetration ones without fighter escort. The P-38 soon proved unequal to coping with enemy fighters and drop-tanks for other Allied fighters were not successful. Priority orders therefore went out to get the North American P-51D long-range Mustang escort into service.

By the end of 1943, therefore, the American strategic bombing effort against Germany, as well as that of the British, was clearly faltering. Hopes were high for 1944, once more technical aids and the long-range fighters became available, but similar visions of forthcoming success had turned out to be false too often before. Such doubts seemed justified in February 1944. The Eighth AAF flew 2688 B-17 and 917 B-24 missions into Germany that month, losing 187 aircraft plus 24 others damaged beyond repair. Within these depressing statistics nestled one gleam of hope: on 29 February 218 B-17s

flew to Brunswick, protected by 654 fighters, including 147 Mustangs. Only one bomber was lost. In the last week of February also, bombers from the US Fifteenth AAF from Italy joined those of the Eighth over Germany.

In March, despite RAF losses during the winter, Harris and the US Commanding General, Lieutenant-General Carl Spaatz, saw themselves on the brink of achieving the 'destruction and dislocation' of German industry, which had been foreseen as long ago as January 1943 by Allied planners. For them, a 'round-the-clock' combined bomber offensive – the Americans by day and the British by night – seemed imminent. Then Operation Overlord – the Allied invasion of occupied France – claimed the attention of 'our most powerful offensive weapon, the heavy bomber force.' Although the bombing of Germany did not entirely stop, between April and September 1944 preparation for the Normandy landings by turning northern France into a 'railway desert,' and the need for post-landing operations against German lines of communication, reduced the strategic bombing effort.

For over five months, therefore, German industry suffered limited, though not negligible, air attack. On 12 May 1944, for example, 935 American bombers attacked and severely damaged six oil plants; 46 bombers were lost, but the Americans proved that they could fight their way through to a precision target. The ghost of Schweinfurt had, at least in part, been laid. And the Mustang was proving its worth. No longer would daylight bomber missions lack long-range fighter cover.

While the Americans were gradually gaining ascendancy over the German defenses by day, at night the RAF was still having serious difficulty. Despite an increasing array of electronic countermeasures, such as the 'Fishpond' radar device to detect fighters, elaborate feint attacks and diversionary raids, in mid-1944 the night-fighter still had the upper hand. Harris, telling the Air Staff that 'remedial action is therefore an urgent oper-

LEFT: B-17Gs of the 94th Bombardment Group, Eighth USAAF, fly in 'combat box' formation, designed to give mutual protection against German day fighters. It enjoyed a measure of success.

RIGHT: B-24s of the 93rd Bombardment Group drop their bombs over Magdeburg, 16 August 1944.

BELOW RIGHT: A B-17, its wing-root ablaze, falls over Berlin, 6 March 1944. The aircraft is from the 482nd Bombardment Group; on board is Brigadier-General Russ Wilson, CO of the 4th Combat Wing. He will not survive.

ational matter which cannot be deferred,' asked for 10 squadrons of long-range Mosquitoes to attack the enemy night-fighters. But the radar equipment issued to these hunters limited their effectiveness, and use of Mosquitoes in this way was not a success. They 'killed' very few enemy fighters.

The newer navigational aids like the Mark II *Gee* were, however, showing their worth for the bombers. But despite the introduction of the Pathfinders and sky marking to overcome poor visibility near the ground, even with *Oboe*, high-altitude marking was still inaccurate. Wing Commander Leonard Cheshire, an experienced bomber pilot, pioneered a system of diving onto a target to mark from low level, and the average main-force error of 700 yards was halved virtually overnight. Together with the use of a Master Bomber to direct aircraft over the target, low-level marking consistently brought very much improved results for night bombing. In the last three months of 1944, 60,000 tons were dropped on the Ruhr and more precise oil and transportation targets were also hit. Between June and August 1944, the loss rate of Bomber Command fell from an average of 11 percent to a more absorbable 3.7 percent. Yet the Ardennes Offensive (the Battle of the Bulge) in December 1944 showed that the Germans were not altogether finished. Emergence of the Messerschmitt Me-262 jet fighter was worrying too. The German fighter 'ace,' Adolph Galland, argued that one of these aircraft was equal to five piston-engined machines. He bitterly regretted Hitler's insistence on making the Me-262 into a bomber; certainly, its speed and maneuverability caused havoc among bomber formations that came into contact with the small number brought into service late in the war.

In January 1945, the Allies agreed to attack, in order, oil, important urban concentrations like Berlin, communications (especially connected with the Ruhr) and jet-aircraft factories. Despite the appearance of the Me-262, Allied bombers now enjoyed virtual air supremacy over Germany. On 3 February 1945, 1000 B-17s attacked Berlin, causing an estimated 25,000 casualties. During the first three months of the year, RAF Bomber Command dropped 87,000 tons of bombs; with the destruction of viaducts at Bielefeld, Arnsberg and Altenbeken, the Ruhr was virtually isolated.

RAF losses were now down to about one percent per raid, and some 1000 four-engined bombers were operating nightly over Germany, with weapons ranging from 20,000lb 'Grand Slam' blockbusters to 4lb incendiaries. Between January and May 1945, Bomber Command and the US Eighth AAF dropped over 370,000 tons of bombs on Germany. In this period, the RAF flew 67,483 sorties for the loss of 608 aircraft, so the bomber did not get through even now completely unscathed. During this time also, the Dresden firestorm raid took place. Harris' reaction to allegations of 'overkill' was not designed to win friends: 'I do not personally regard the whole of the remaining cities of Germany as worth the bones of one British Grenadier.' In a macabre sense, he was articulating one of the main reasons for the promotion of strategic bombing: air forces could save casualties in the trenches by paralyzing the enemy war effort at source – in the heart of the enemy's industrial homeland.

Only extreme protagonists of strategic bombing truly believed that it could win the war against Germany unaided. Undoubtedly, though, at least in the final stages, strategic bombing did make a substantial contribution to Allied victory. By April 1945, Germany's capacity to wage war had indeed been 'fatally undermined' through persistent aerial attacks by day and night, as Allied command of the air allowed. That position of superiority was not fully achieved until the closing months of the war in Europe. Then, daylight precision attacks became possible for both the American and British bombers. The hopes of prewar enthusiasts had thus been realized.

It should not be forgotten either that, until 1944, strategic bombing was the only means of putting direct pressure on the enemy homeland and, in so doing, it raised the morale of Allied civilians who had themselves suffered aerial bombardment. To that extent, strategic bombing might not have adversely affected enemy morale to a large degree – available evidence points to a stiffening of German morale in much the same way that occurred in England during the Blitz – but the simple fact of its pursuit most certainly enhanced that of the Allies.

RAF Bomber Command lost 55,573 aircrew and 1570 ground staff in the course of the strategic bombing offensive against Germany. Including casualties among the escorting fighters, the US Eighth AAF recorded 43,742 dead and 1923 seriously wounded. 'Round-the-clock' bombing by British and American aircraft may not have been fully effective until the final phase of the war, but however imperfectly it was carried out and however limited its physical achievements in terms of crucial damage to the German war machine, in the years since 1939 it had made a very considerable overall contribution to the Allied war effort. Two inescapable lessons emerged from the air war over Germany. First, the bomber would get through only when enemy defenses were negligible. Second, bombing tended to stiffen, not destroy, civilian morale. Both should have been made obvious by the experience of the Luftwaffe during the Blitz on England in 1940-41. Such is the futility of war.

RIGHT: B-24J Liberator 'Little Warrior' of the 493rd Bombardment Group burns after having been hit by anti-aircraft fire over Quakenbrück, 29 June 1944. The aircraft is about to explode.

BELOW LEFT: Bomb damage to Nuremberg, 1945. Although the RAF suffered one of its worst loss rates over this city in late March 1944, it was badly hit in that and other raids.

BELOW: Stockyards at Leipzig are destroyed by the Ninth USAAF, May 1945. In the closing stages of the war in Europe, enemy communications targets were a primary objective.

THE BOMBING
OF JAPAN

War came to the Pacific on Sunday 7 December 1941. At 0755 hours, Japanese bombers and dive-bombers began to attack the American fleet anchored at Pearl Harbor, on the Hawaiian island of Oahu; shortly afterward torpedo-planes also launched their deadly weapons toward the eight battleships and many smaller warships. Flying in two separate waves, 353 aircraft from Admiral Chuichi Nagumo's task force of six carriers destroyed 311 American aircraft (mostly on the ground), sank two battleships and immobilized another three, all in a mere 37 minutes.

Nagumo's preemptive strike aimed to cripple American naval power and prevent effective interference with Japanese plans to conquer Southeast Asia. Despite the severe damage, it failed to do so, principally because the two American aircraft carriers, *Enterprise* and *Lexington*, were not in port at the time of the attack. In an indirect way, too, it showed how failure to neutralize an enemy's industrial power could jeopardize hopes of eventual success. Nagumo struck at American military might; he did not affect the vast manufacturing base in the USA. Learning of the unprovoked attack, delivered without warning, Winston Churchill recalled a remark made by former British Foreign Secretary Edward Grey: the United States was like 'a gigantic boiler. Once the fire is lighted under it there is no limit to the power it can generate.'

Like the citizens of London, suffering under aerial attack from German bombers in both 1917 and 1940, the American people demanded swift retaliatory action. A bomber raid on Tokyo, launched from carriers in the Pacific, was the only feasible option. No Allied airfields were in range of the Japanese capital.

A former aeronautical engineer, experienced long-distance airman and currently a staff officer in Washington, Lieutenant-Colonel James H Doolittle, volunteered to lead the mission. Doolittle chose 24 crews of the 17th Bombardment Group USAAF for training in Florida. They would fly the twin-engined North American B-25 Mitchell, equipped with extra fuel tanks. Loaded with three 500lb bombs and an incendiary cluster, each aircraft would attack at low level, then fly to friendly bases in China.

Sixteen B-25s were therefore secured on the flight-deck of the carrier USS *Hornet*, protected by a task force of another aircraft carrier, four cruisers and eight destroyers. The plan was to launch the bombers 450 miles west of Japan, which left them another 650 miles to the Chinese airfields after hitting the target. Unluckily, the naval task force was sighted by enemy forces on the morning of 18 April 1942, some 10 hours before the planned night attack. Doolittle decided to take off immediately, even though he was 823 miles from Tokyo. To make matters worse, *Hornet* was pitching violently in a 40-knot gale. That every B-25 successfully became airborne was, in itself, a minor miracle.

Doolittle's force achieved complete surprise. Attacking at 1000 feet, the B-25s dropped bombs on industrial and military installations not only in Tokyo, but also in Kobe, Yokohama and Nagoya. One bomb hit the aircraft carrier

PAGES 50-51: The remains of Hiroshima, photographed in early 1946, some months after the devastating atomic raid by the Americans. Instantaneous destruction and 78,000 deaths were the results.

BELOW LEFT: US engineers and seamen struggle to save trapped crew members of the capsized battleship USS *Oklahoma* in the aftermath of the Japanese air attack on Pearl Harbor, December 1941.

RIGHT: Lieutenant-Colonel James Doolittle's force of specially modified B-25 Mitchell bombers prepares to take off from the deck of the carrier USS *Hornet* to bomb Tokyo, 18 April 1942.

Ryuho in dry-dock, and Doolittle justifiably signaled: 'Damage far exceeded that most optimistic expectations.' Only one Mitchell was damaged, by antiaircraft fire. But, due to the extreme range at which they were launched from *Hornet*, all 16 bombers failed to reach the allotted airfields in China. Several crews baled out and lived; others crashlanded along the Chinese coast. The Japanese captured eight airmen and executed three of them for the deliberate bombing of civilians; a ninth airman died parachuting into China. Their fate could not dampen public enthusiasm for Doolittle's feat. He survived to receive the Medal of Honor – America's highest award for bravery – and went on to attain high command later in the war.

For all its morale value, the Doolittle Raid achieved nothing of long-term value. In fact, it served to underline an American inability to launch air strikes of any real consequence against Japan. At the time of Pearl Harbor, the United States had only 159 four-engined bombers in service. Even if they were all committed to hitting Japan, there were no Allied airfields within range to do so, and to launch them from a carrier like the B-25s was simply impossible – no carriers existed that were big enough to accommodate heavy bombers.

Yet there was pressure for an air offensive against Japan. Strategic bombing theory was persuasive in this respect, for in July 1941 the Air War Plans Division in Washington had penned words of which Billy Mitchell would have approved: 'If the air offensive is successful, a land offensive may not be necessary.' And a weapon was being developed which could attack Japan – the Boeing B-29 Superfortress bomber. Moreover, Admiral Chester W Nimitz (Commander of the Pacific Fleet from 31 December 1941) argued strongly that the aerial cam-

paign against Germany was 'of no use': the Pacific was the crucial theater for the United States.

Before the United States entered the war, Lieutenant-General Henry H Arnold, then Deputy Chief of Staff (Air), told aeronautical engineers designing heavy bombers to 'make them the biggest, gun them the heaviest and fly them the farthest.' It would take five years before the first B-29 went into combat. Plans to produce a 'very long range bomber' were approved in December 1939 and tenders requested from various aircraft manufacturing companies. In May 1940 the Boeing Aircraft Company's design for a flying monster was chosen: it was to have a wingspan of 141 feet, a fuselage 93 feet long, a range of 7000 miles, a top speed of 382mph at 25,000 feet and a bomb-carrying capacity of 2000lbs. For protection, the plane would carry 10 0.50in machine guns and a 20mm cannon in the tail. After further design and experimental work, Boeing received a contract in September 1940.

At that time, American direct involvement in the European war seemed unlikely and many alterations in design took place without the pressure of impending action during the ensuing months. The gross weight of the new machine posed a major problem – at 98,000lbs it was over twice the weight of the B-17. Difficulties also occurred with developing pressurized crew accommodation in an aircraft whose two large bomb-bay doors would be frequently opened and closed. And the engines – four newly developed Wright R-3350 Cyclones – proved to be underpowered. Nor were these the only innovations. A small automatic gunnery computer was planned to correct for range, altitude, temperature and airspeed; there was also a central fire control mechanism which allowed any gunner except the rear one to take control of more than one of the five power-driven turrets. All but the rear gunner fired from remote positions, so that they could more easily track enemy fighters without the distraction of vibration and recoil experienced when in direct contact with the guns. The many additions, like pressurization and fire control systems, required special generating equipment. In the end, despite removal of unnecessary items, the gross weight actually reached 105,000lbs.

In the wake of Pearl Harbor, an order was placed for 500 of these planes, even before the prototype had flown. Two months later, 1600 were ordered and production of them given to four companies – Boeing, General Motors, North American Aviation and the Bell Aircraft Corporation. Each would specialize in specific components, which would then be assembled at other designated centers. Necessary speed of production dictated such a complicated arrangement. In spite of the many early snags, at length the prototype took to the air on 21 September 1942. Arnold, now Chief of the Army Air Forces, declared enthusiastically that this plane would lead to Japan's surrender. Initial reactions from the test pilots were also favorable: 'Unbelievable for such a large plane to be so easy to control' . . . 'stall characteristics remarkable for such a heavy plane.'

Throughout the winter of 1942-43, further test flights were undertaken. Then, on 18 February 1943, the second prototype crashed, killing all those on board. Production slowed while a full investigation took place. Even when test flights resumed, the engines still gave trouble, and their problems had not been fully solved when the aircraft went to war. They did so in the Far East.

The Doolittle Raid had prompted the Japanese troops in China to drive inland, capturing airfields from which the B-17 or B-24 might hit Japan. In January 1943 President Roosevelt, in an effort to boost Chinese morale, supported the 'periodic bombing of Japan.' Bombers would be based in India, refueling in China to and from their targets in Japan. This would remove the need for 'tremendously expensive' support facilities in China. Seven months later, the first production models of the B-29 came off the assembly lines and, at the Allied 'Quadrant' Conference in Canada in August 1943, the Americans proposed that B-29s, given their 1500-mile operational range, could mount a prolonged campaign to cripple Japanese factories from China. This was classic strategic bombing theory: flying five missions a month, 780 B-29s would destroy the base of Japanese war production. It all seemed little more than fantasy when only 16 of the 97 bombers that came off the assembly lines in January 1944 were mechanically trouble-free. In December 1943, however, the Chinese Nationalist leader, Chiang Kai-shek, had agreed that B-29s could not only make use of Chinese airfields but be stationed permanently on them. Japan was now very much in range and there was no going back.

Mainly through Arnold's personal energy, the first B-29s reached 20th Bomber Command in India in April 1944, though mechanical troubles still plagued the small force. At last, on 5 June, they flew their first combat mission, not to Japan, but to lightly defended railway marshaling yards at Bangkok in Thailand. Of the 98 bombers that took off, only 48 attacked, from 17-27,000 feet using radar through cloud and haze. Of these, a mere 18 actually bombed anywhere near the target. Five B-29s were lost that day, none from enemy action. The 20th's commander, Major-General Kenneth B Wolfe, nevertheless came under heavy pressure from Washington to attack Japan without delay.

So, on 18 June, 75 B-29s took off from Chinese bases near Chengtu for a 3200-mile round trip to the iron and steel works at Yawata on the southernmost Japanese island of Kyushu, which reputedly produced 24 percent of Japan's rolled steel. The raid was timed to take place shortly before midnight, the aircraft flying singly instead of in formation. Due to mechanical failures and early returns, only 63 Superfortresses actually crossed the enemy coast and, contrary to expectations, radar did detect their approach. The city was blacked out, fighter, searchlight and antiaircraft defenses alert. Forty-seven bombers claimed to have attacked the target, believing that they caused 'considerable damage' to the steel works. In fact, just one bomb fell in the vicinity – on a power-house three-quarters of a mile away. Eight B-29s were lost, although again none of them to enemy action. However imperfectly, though, the strategic bombing of Japan had commenced. An enemy source admitted that the attack 'sent a ripple of apprehension throughout the main islands of Japan.' Wolfe declared that this was 'but the beginning of the organized destruction of the Japanese industrial empire.'

But the failure at Yawata lost Wolfe his job. Major-General Curtis E LeMay (known for his determination in Europe as 'Old Iron Ass') took over. Like Air Marshal Harris on assuming command of the RAF bombing effort in February 1942, LeMay had to prove the bombing potential of his aircraft quickly, for the navy wanted bombers to support their operations in the Pacific. Arriving in August 1944, LeMay flew a mission to Manchuria on 8 September, declared the enemy defenses less than lethal and promptly set about improving efficiency. Individual flying would stop: the bombers would go in formation

BELOW: Major-General Curtis E LeMay was appointed to command the B-29s in China in August 1944.

TOP RIGHT: A Boeing B-29 Superfortress takes on fuel. Its Wright R-3350-23 Cyclone engines were a constant source of trouble.

ABOVE RIGHT: One of the B-29 prototypes is inspected by service and civilian experts.

wind, now let it reap the whirlwind,' he exclaimed.

Despite the technical advantages of the Superfortress, destruction of Japanese industry from the Marianas was by no means easy. The flight involved twice the distance of any in the European theater, almost all of it over water and within range of Japanese territory. A minor navigational error could spell death for a crew that would thus miss its base or run out of fuel. The 21st found that strong winds (the 'jet stream') and thick cloud were often encountered over Japan, so that vital identification of the targets from the bombing height of 20-35,000 feet proved difficult. Bombing accuracy left much to be desired.

Seven further raids on aircraft factories in Tokyo and Nagoya in November-December 1944 thus had only marginal effect. Moreover, mechanical problems were still causing too many aircraft to turn back, while enemy defenses began to take a worrying toll of the attacking bombers. At the end of the year, Hansell admitted that results were 'far from the standards we are seeking.' Drawing attention to the difficulties caused by weather, he went on more specifically: 'We have not put all our bombs exactly where we wanted to put them and therefore we are not by any means satisfied with what we have done so far.' He concluded: 'We are still in our early, experimental stages.'

Hansell's cautious conclusions did not impress Arnold, who replaced him in January 1945 with LeMay in a search for more positive thought. LeMay increased training and introduced the system of lead crews for navigation purposes which he had used in Europe and with the 20th Bomber Command in China. He also stepped up the number of B-29s flying on missions against Nagoya and Tokyo to 100 and, on 25 February, sent 200 to drop 600 tons of bombs on the Japanese capital. He was already using 'jellied gasoline-magnesium incendiaries' (an early form of napalm, recently developed) as well as high explosive.

At the beginning of March, LeMay took stock of the situation. It was not, he decided, promising. B-29s from the Marianas (now including Guam as well as Saipan) were flying a 15-hour round trip to Tokyo. Due to fuel needs, only some 5000lbs of bombs could be carried and the poor visibility, which Hansell had already experienced, further reduced the effectiveness of high-level daylight bombing, which relied on visual identification of targets. Quite often, bombs were simply being dumped in the general area of a target. LeMay concluded that a lot of effort was therefore being 'thrown away.'

He decided to send out even larger formations, arm them with incendiaries and bomb from 5-8000 feet. He reasoned that at this low altitude, visual identification would always be possible, as high clouds had been a major problem to date. He argued that low-level attacks would also frustrate the Japanese antiaircraft defenses, geared for high-level action. Even more controversially, LeMay decided to send the B-29s to Japan unarmed to allow greater speed, a heavier bomb and fuel load. Speed would be the B-29s' defense. Additional protection against prowling fighters would be given by darkness for, as the British had found in 1940, the bomber had a better chance of survival at night. Flares would illuminate the target.

In fact, night area bombing had replaced daylight precision attacks. The aim was now to burn whole urban

(similar to the combat 'box' system introduced by LeMay over Germany) and bomb on the leader's signal. On 26 September, LeMay despatched 73 B-29s to the Japanese steel plant at Anshan in Manchuria. Little damage was done, but importantly for morale, no aircraft were lost. LeMay then abandoned night attacks in favor of high-level daylight missions − with which he had been familiar in Europe. Twice during October, the Okayama aircraft assembly works on Formosa (Taiwan) were attacked in this way. With limited strength, LeMay nonetheless mounted an average of four missions a month from China during late 1944, including three on the Omura aircraft assembly plant on Kyushu.

Meanwhile, the first B-29s of the 21st Bomber Command under Brigadier-General Haywood S Hansell had arrived on Saipan, one of the Mariana Islands, some 1450 miles southeast of Tokyo. On 1 November 1944, a single B-29 flew a reconnaissance mission from Saipan over the Japanese capital. Then, on 24 November, 94 B-29s of the 21st attacked the Nakajima aircraft plant in Tokyo. Only 24 even claimed to have bombed the briefed target: 57 Japanese were killed and 75 injured, but little damage was caused to the plant. Nevertheless, in Washington Arnold was delighted that Tokyo had again been hit − this time much harder than by Doolittle's token effort. He argued that Japanese industry was now vulnerable to the B-29s' might: 'Japan has sowed the

centers, as a preponderance of incendiaries were also to be carried. To counter anticipated objections from strategic bombing purists at home, LeMay explained that Japanese industry relied on a multitude of small factories scattered throughout large urban concentrations like Tokyo, Kobe, Nagoya and Osaka. Thus, the middle of cities must be the aiming point. Already several 'test' incendiary raids had been carried out, though LeMay's predecessor had protested against the order to mount them, maintaining that 'our mission is the destruction of primary targets by sustained and determined attacks using precision bombing methods.' A senior officer, Lieutenant-General Millard F Harmon, commander of all AAF units in the Pacific, similarly held that 'burning flimsy houses will not beat the Japs. Our targets are war industries.' Now, though, LeMay could point to a directive from Twentieth Air Force Headquarters dated 19 February, which made area attacks on cities a priority in the drive to eliminate the enemy aircraft industry. High-altitude incendiary raids, like that on Tokyo on 25 February, and so-called precision attacks were simply not working.

On the night of 9/10 March, LeMay launched a full-scale night area attack on Tokyo. A total of 385 B-29s, carrying 2000 tons of incendiaries, took off at dusk; 279 of them reached the target area to find that markers had been dropped by pathfinder aircraft. Ten square miles of the Japanese capital, officially 'crammed' with small factories, were soon alight. For two hours, more incendiaries rained on the growing conflagration, as smaller fires merged into one immense blaze. A firestorm, like those created by the RAF at Hamburg and Dresden, took effect. High winds further fanned the leaping flames. A Japanese commentator explained: 'The city was as bright as sunrise; clouds of smoke, soot, even sparks driven by the storm, were flying over it. That night we thought the whole of Tokyo was reduced to ashes.'

Once the embers had cooled, the scale of destruction became all too evident. Sixteen, not 10 square miles had been gutted; 25 percent of Tokyo's buildings razed. 124,701 casualties (including 83,783 dead) occurred on the ground; in all some one million people became homeless. Fourteen bombers were lost, although the crews of five that ditched in the sea were subsequently saved.

Two days later, 286 B-29s attacked the aircraft production complex at Nagoya, dropping 1950 tons of incendiaries from 5000 feet. The theory that flimsy Japanese houses would burn easily seemed well founded, and the mini-blitz continued. In the early hours of 14 March, 280 B-29s used 2240 tons of incendiaries to devastate eight square miles of Japan's third largest port, Osaka. Three square miles of Kobe similarly suffered on 17 March, and the untouched areas of Nagoya were scorched two days afterward. In 10 days, B-29s destroyed an estimated 32 square miles of Japan's four largest cities. During the rest of the month, the net was spread wider, although Nagoya and Tokyo in particular did not escape added attention.

In the United States, staff officers referred to these attacks as 'the initial phase' of the B-29 intention to undermine the enemy war effort. LeMay was singled out for praise 'for solving an acute operational problem by using high altitude Superfortresses at low level to achieve the unloading of a large tonnage of bombs in a short time.' Unfortunately, in doing so, he had virtually exhausted 21st Bomber Command's stock of incendiaries by the end of March 1945. No more major fire raids would be possible for a time, and this lull coincided with B-29s being diverted to support the amphibious assault on Okinawa.

By mid-April, however, LeMay's command had been reinforced to allow planning for missions of 500 bombers, and his ammunition supplies had been replenished. So, when the bombers were at length released from their invasion support role on 11 May, LeMay could confidently predict that the 21st would destroy the Japanese war economy, 'provided its maximum capacity is exerted unstintingly during the next six months.' He set out to prove his point.

On 14 May, 472 B-29s flew in daylight to Nagoya, where 2500 tons of incendiaries ostensibly aimed at the Mitsubishi plant destroyed three square miles of the city. But 11 bombers were lost and another 54 damaged. Two days later, another 3600 tons fell on Nagoya and a further four square miles suffered. An estimated 200,000 people fled the city as a result of these two raids. On 23 May, Tokyo came under attack yet again. At night 520 Superfortresses dropped 3600 tons of incendiaries, harassed by 60 fighters and heavy antiaircraft fire. Seventeen B-29s were lost and 69 damaged. Two days later, another 500 bombers dropped 3200 tons; this time, 26 were shot down. Even the Superfortresses were proving uncomfortably vulnerable.

So, on 29 May, LeMay reverted to a high-level precision assault by day on the port of Yokohama. More than 150 enemy fighters lay in wait for the 454 bombers, but a nasty surprise was in store for them. The attackers were protected by long-range P-51 Mustangs from the island of Iwo Jima, now in American hands. The lessons of Europe had been reabsorbed. Over 2500 tons of incendiaries fell on Yokohama, devastating seven square miles for the loss of only four B-29s. In a similar attack on Osaka on 1 June, 2700 tons cleared three square miles of the city. This time, though, bad weather disrupted concentration of the Mustang escort and five B-29s went down. The American fighter defense was better coordinated four days later at Kobe, where four square miles and some 52,000 buildings were destroyed for the loss of

LEFT: Bomb damage to Tokyo, 1945 – a photograph taken after some initial clearing up has taken place.

RIGHT: A B-29 Superfortress, suffering a serious oil leak from No 3 engine, flies over the Japanese industrial area of Osaka, 1 June 1945. Below, the target is burning.

three B-29s. By mid-June, an estimated 40 percent of Japan's six largest cities had been wiped out.

On 17 June, LeMay began a series of simultaneous night incendiary attacks on smaller cities, with one by 450 B-29s against Kagoshima, Omuta, Hamamatsu and Yokkaichi. Soon, he added a psychological dimension, sending a few planes to drop leaflets announcing that a number of towns would be bombed. On 27 July, for example, 11 cities were on the list, and the following night six were attacked with 3700 tons of incendiaries. A similar exercise was carried out on 1 and 4 August. As one Japanese industrialist admitted: 'The leaflets had a great effect on the morale of the people. They figured if the enemy could announce a raid beforehand, the enemy was superior.'

Between March and August 1945, therefore, LeMay's B-29s pounded Japan with high explosive and incendiaries. Whole areas of its cities were laid waste quite dramatically with thousands of tons of bombs — a vast improvement on Doolittle's 15 tons of three years previously. Yet, despite this overwhelming onslaught, Japanese morale did not crack, nor was the industrial might of the country completely undermined. The need to invade the Japanese home islands, with an estimated casualty rate of over one million Allied soldiers, still loomed uncomfortably large in future planning. That is, until the B-29 found a new, decisive weapon to drop.

Early in July 1945, Winston Churchill backed President Harry Truman's decision that the atomic bombs, which were close to completion, should be used against Japan. Already, Colonel Paul W Tibbets had taken command of the 509th Composite Group, whose B-29s were modified and its crews specially trained to drop the new

ABOVE LEFT: Japanese midget submarines lie destroyed in Kure harbor, Japan, 1945. In addition to industrial targets, the B-29s also aimed to destroy Japan's war-making capability.

LEFT: A photograph, taken in 1946, shows the destruction inflicted on the business district of Kobe by the B-29s. Some reconstruction is already evident.

ABOVE RIGHT: Incendiary bombs rain down on Kobe during a B-29 raid on 4 June 1945. The pall of smoke tells its own story of the devastation below.

RIGHT: Smoke pours from burning buildings and dockyard facilities in Osaka in the aftermath of a B-29 attack, 1 June 1945.

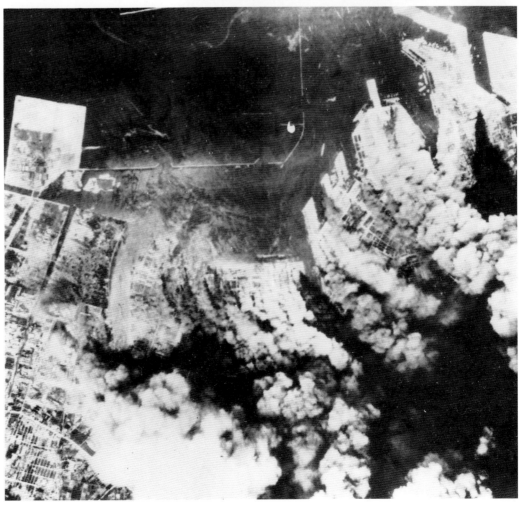

weapon. That month, July 1945, the 509th arrived at North Field Air Base on Tinian in the Marianas. While it continued intensive training, a successful test explosion took place in the New Mexico desert, described by one awestruck observer: 'A huge ball of fire was formed which lasted several seconds . . . (and then) mushroomed and rose to a height of over 10,000 feet.'

Knowing of the successful test, the Allied leaders meeting at Potsdam called upon Japan to surrender or face 'prompt and utter destruction.' The Japanese publicly announced that they would 'ignore' this call and 'resolutely fight for the successful conclusion of the war.' So at 0816 hours on 6 August, piloted by Tibbets, the B-29 *Enola Gay* dropped the first atomic bomb (code-named 'Little Boy'), slowed by parachute to allow the bomber to clear the target area safely, from five miles above Hiroshima. In less than a millisecond, as the bomb exploded, 78,000 people were killed, 51,000 injured and 176,000 made homeless. Some 48,000 buildings were destroyed and 22,000 damaged.

Truman once more called on the Japanese to surrender, otherwise steps would be taken to 'obliterate ... every productive enterprise' in Japan. 'Let there be no mistake,' he continued, 'we shall completely destroy Japan's power to make war.' Much the same threats had been made by strategic bombing theorists for years, so the Japanese hesitated. Leaflets were scattered far and wide over Japan by American aircraft, underlining the fate of Hiroshima: 'You should take steps now to cease military resistance. Otherwise we shall resolutely employ this bomb and all our other superior weapons to promptly and forcefully end the war.'

Still the Japanese politicians could not agree. So, just after 1100 hours on 9 August, a second atomic bomb exploded over Nagasaki. Another 35,000 people were killed and 60,000 injured. Next day, the Japanese sued for peace. They were not to know that the Allies had no more atomic bombs available.

ABOVE, FAR LEFT: The atomic bomb nicknamed 'Little Boy.'

ABOVE LEFT: Colonel Paul W Tibbetts, CO of the 509th Composite Group, poses in front of his B-29 'Enola Gay.'

LEFT: B-29 'Enola Gay' – the world's first atomic bomber.

ABOVE: The atomic bomb nicknamed 'Fat Man,' used against Nagasaki on 9 August 1945.

ABOVE RIGHT: The distinctive mushroom cloud of dust and debris blown up to 10,000ft above Hiroshima in the first few minutes after the atomic explosion, 6 August 1945.

RIGHT: Hiroshima after the atomic attack.

The two atomic bombs were decisive, therefore. But they came at the end of a powerful strategic bombing campaign, in which B-29s flew 34,790 sorties to drop 170,000 tons of bombs on Japan. The raids of 6 and 9 August 1945 should be seen as part of this campaign. Arguably, bombing did at length undermine the enemy's will to continue the war, but it should be remembered that the island-hopping advance by American forces in the Pacific, the destruction of Japan's merchant shipping fleet by submarines and mines, and the Soviet declaration of war early on 9 August (followed by an invasion of Manchuria) all played an equally significant part. Attractive though it might seem, strategic bombing alone did not win the war. The atomic bombs suggested, however, that it might do so in the future. The elusive knock-out blow seemed closer to reality.

LEFT: The mushroom cloud over Nagasaki, 9 August 1945. About 35,000 people have just died.

RIGHT: Few buildings could withstand the blast of an atomic explosion: these in Japan are merely shells.

BELOW: Devastation caused by one of the atomic explosions, August 1945: such levels of instantaneous devastation seemed to vindicate the prewar bombing theorists.

BELOW RIGHT: Crewmen on board the battleship USS *Missouri* watch as the Japanese delegation arrives to sign the surrender, Tokyo Bay, 2 September 1945.

THE POSTWAR WORLD

In the immediate aftermath of the World War II bombing campaigns against Germany and Japan, an independent United States Air Force (USAF) was founded. Perhaps even more significantly, a Strategic Air Command (SAC), comprising aircraft capable of delivering nuclear or conventional bombs to long-distance targets also evolved. The frightening demonstrations of airpower at Hiroshima and Nagasaki had apparently proved beyond doubt that Douhet, Trenchard, Mitchell and a host of other strategic bombing supporters were right after all.

In the post-1945 world, the heavy bomber would play two distinct roles in strategic thinking. As a vehicle for the delivery of atomic weapons, it would form an integral part in the concept of nuclear deterrence, itself very much a development of traditional strategic bombing theory. The mere threat of a nuclear strike would deter an enemy from taking hostile action. If he did so, a devastating reply awaited him. Mutually Assured Destruction (MAD) would, by the mid-1960s, become the bedrock of nuclear deterrence, whereby each potential opponent would have the capability to annihilate the other. Yet within this whole area of thought lurked an old idea – the knock-out blow disguised in the new terminology as a 'first strike.' With his political and industrial base destroyed, the enemy could no longer threaten. A far cry from the RAF's Western Air Plans of 1937, with planned attacks on the Ruhr industry of Germany, but at root little different in principle.

Despite the technological advances which added yet more sophisticated missile delivery systems for nuclear weapons, the manned bomber has never been entirely replaced. In fact, all heavy bombers to date have retained a conventional as well as nuclear capability. Thus, the capacity for launching a conventional strategic bombing campaign still exists.

Planners, though, even today would be foolish to ignore the lessons from 1939-45. The knock-out blow, or preemptive aerial attack, at the outset of war with Germany and Japan did not materialize. This was partly because no side had the ability to launch such a decisive assault and, perhaps more crucially, defenses had not stood still. One major flaw in pre-1939 thinking was that the attacking bomber would always get through, because it would do so virtually unopposed. Any minor irritations would be dealt with by powerful self-defending machines. However, over Germany and Japan, the bomber forces learnt that daylight attacks were costly and that night raids, at least in the initial stages of applying that tactic, cost fewer planes. The penalty was lack of accuracy: Harris and LeMay both, therefore, resorted to area attacks on cities. Yet once more, the defenses did not lag far behind in technological development: the German night-fighters, for instance, soon began to pose a very real threat to the RAF, as their daylight counterparts were decimating US crews. The daylight solution was production of long-range fighter escorts. At night, installation of more and more electronic aids in the bombers to detect incoming fighter attacks only provided a partial solution. The Mosquito, adapted to seek out enemy fighters at night, was never satisfactory.

One extreme tenet of strategic bombing theory was unquestioningly refuted: that air forces would reduce the other two services to a secondary role, if not actually make them obsolete. In 1945, almost 3500 British and American heavy bombers were pounding Germany. They reduced extensive areas to rubble, yet overall they killed less than 0.5 percent of Germans and failed to crack enemy morale. Nor was the effect on German industry so dramatic. The RAF believed that the produc-

PAGES 64-65: An Avro Vulcan B Mark 2 in low-level camouflage is accompanied by a similar aircraft in the original all-white finish, 1964. Designed and deployed as an atomic bomber, the Vulcan saw action only once – as a conventional bomber over the Falklands in 1982.

LEFT: A Boeing B-52D Stratofortress bomber of the type used by the Americans in Vietnam, 1965-72. Internal modifications allowed each B-52 to carry over 67,000lbs of conventional bombs.

RIGHT: An Avro Vulcan B Mark 2 of the type used on the RAF's 'Black Buck' raids from Ascension Island to Port Stanley in the Falklands, May-June 1982.

tion of single-seater fighters had been cut by 40 percent in 1944; actually it rose in that year. The American raids on Schweinfurt were doomed to failure, whatever their physical impact on the five target factories. Ball-bearing production had already been dispersed throughout Germany, supplies could be obtained from neutral manufacturers like SKF of Sweden, and the Germans soon discovered that there were more stocks available in store than hitherto realized. The Combined Bomber Offensive certainly did make a tremendous contribution to the crushing of Nazi resistance, but it had its most effective impact once ground forces had begun their last advances on Germany from east and west. Arguments that only 10 percent of the Allied war effort had been devoted to the bombing campaigns and therefore that the theory had never been given a fair trial, show amazing naivety. No government could have risked allocating the bulk of its resources to an unproven theory. Technically, in any case, the means to achieve success were not to hand. Any number of twin-engined bombers in 1940 would not have allowed the RAF to devastate the Ruhr.

To some extent, the lessons of Germany were underlined in the case of Japan. Before the atomic bombs were dropped, almost 2.5 million Japanese houses had been destroyed, together with the overwhelming majority of business premises in the industrial areas of 60 cities and large towns. Over 500,000 Japanese had been killed or seriously injured. Yet, as with Germany, morale did not break. The relentless advance of American troops toward Japan through the Pacific islands was similar in effect to the landward advance of the Allies across Europe. In both cases, of course, a strong naval blockade was also in force, further weakening the Axis powers.

The truth was, therefore, that conventional strategic bombing campaigns had not provided a decisive inde-

pendent contribution to warfare. The likelihood was that it never would. However, the capacity to carry out non-nuclear attacks by heavy bombers remained a priority. The US Strategic Air Command argued that all the aircraft it sponsored after the B-29 up to and beyond the B-52 must have both a nuclear and conventional capability. The eight-engined Boeing B-52 Stratofortress turbojet entered service in 1955 as a high-level bomber. In the 1960s, the B-52G model carried a crew of six, had a maximum speed of 630mph at 24,000 feet and a ceiling of 55,000 feet. In the remotely controlled rear turret were four 0.50in machine guns, its bomb-load totaled 27,000lb and it also carried two Hound Dog air-to-ground missiles. Operational experience in Vietnam in the mid-to-late 1960s led to modification of the bomb-bay to allow the B-52D (nicknamed BUFF – Big Ugly Fat Fellow – due to its large belly) either internally or on pylon racks under the wings to carry a massive 67,500 lbs. This load replaced the original B-52 specification for two thermo-nuclear weapons. B-29s of SAC were used in a non-nuclear role in the Korean War (1950-53), the B-52s in Vietnam (1965-72).

The RAF followed a similar line of thought. Its V-Bombers (principally the Avro Vulcan) also came into service in the mid-1950s primarily with a nuclear role in view. But, subsequently, they too were modified to carry conventional loads. As such, they were used during the brief Suez campaign of 1956 and the Falklands conflict of 1982. Since 1945, however, the United Kingdom has not attempted to launch a conventional strategic bombing campaign and no longer has a heavy bomber in its strategic arsenal.

Thus the main evidence for the continuing relevance of strategic bombing theory comes from American experience. Purists may hold that neither Korea nor Viet-

LEFT: Britain's 'V-Bomber' force (left to right: Vulcan, Valiant and Victor) was developed and deployed in the 1950s to deliver atomic weapons.

RIGHT: The results of a B-29 raid on the Pyongyang rail marshaling yards, North Korea, August 1950.

BELOW: President Harry Truman (left) and General Douglas MacArthur, photographed in October 1950. Early the following year, MacArthur was to be sacked for advocating a tougher response to Communist attacks in Korea.

BELOW RIGHT: Damage inflicted by B-29s on the Konan chemical-industrial complex in North Korea.

nam had either the urban concentrations or industrial capacity to permit an effective bombing campaign. They may well have a point, but these two wars were conducted with political constraint very much in the minds of statesmen. Unrestricted bombing would have escalated the conflict, especially if, as the American General Douglas MacArthur advocated, it were carried out beyond the confines of the existing war zone.

In Korea, the lack of suitable targets did partly ensure that the B-29s could not mount a conventional strategic bombing campaign, even though the political necessity to fight a limited war also carried considerable weight. Primarily, the heavy bombers were employed to hit tactical (battlefield) or theater (battle-zone) targets. In November 1950 MacArthur, the commander of United Nations forces in Korea, ordered the bombers 'to destroy every means of communication and every installation, factory, city and village' in North Korea, and to cut bridges over the Yalu River border with Manchuria to discourage direct Chinese intervention in the war. When this failed, he pressed for bombing across the border against the industrial base of the enemy – China – which had now invaded from the north.

This was refused for political reasons and thereafter during the war the B-29s were employed to hit theater targets such as supply dumps and bridges in Communist-occupied territory. Once more, lessons of a previous war had to be relearnt. Early in 1951, B-29s attacked new Chinese airfields south of the Yalu in daylight. Despite a fighter escort, they suffered heavy losses, and resort was then made to nighttime raids. But still attacks on cities were forbidden for fear of unnecessary escalation. In June 1952, the Superfortresses were unleashed on the Suiho hydro-electric plants along the Yalu to good effect – in three days 90 percent of North Korea's supplies were halted; in May 1953 raids were carried out on irrigation dams at Toksan and Chasan. During the Korean War,

B-29s flew 21,328 combat missions and dropped 167,000 tons of bombs. By no stretch of the imagination did they bring that conflict to a close, nor did they in any sense undertake a strategic offensive of their own. Like those who complained that not enough effort had gone into the campaign against Germany during World War II, the continuing belief that manned bombers carrying conventional bomb-loads had the ability to win wars was summarized by one commentator: 'The objective was to win a truce, not the complete military victory which American airpower was capable of gaining.'

Twelve years after the end of the Korean conflict came the American involvement in Vietnam. Once more, fear of escalation exercised the minds of statesmen and politicians. In February 1965, two B-52 Wings were concentrated on Guam. Four months later, they became in-

volved in the war when they were called on to carry out bombing raids over South Vietnam known as Arc Light. They acted, however, against tactical targets only. On 18 June 1965, 30 B-52s hit Viet Cong (VC) bases in Binh Duong Province, north of Saigon, from high level. Visual identification proved difficult in the broken terrain and little damage was inflicted. Tactical strikes of this nature were continued and improved bombing techniques adopted. Missions were coordinated from airborne bombing directors over the targets – similar in concept to the RAF Master Bombers of World War II. Radar bombing, not requiring visual identification, was also used more routinely. But while Guam remained the main base for the B-52s, time over the target was limited, so in April 1967 U-Tapao in Thailand was made available, which vastly reduced flying time. By then, the use of B-52s in Arc Light operations was a feature of the conflict, with American and South Vietnamese soldiers on the ground used to the rumble of B-52 strikes, delivered from such an altitude that the bombers could be neither seen nor heard as they approached. A cell of three B-52s could drop nearly 200,000lbs of high explosive, devastating the target area; the effect on the morale of VC or North Vietnamese troops caught in such an area – as they were around the besieged US Marine base at Khe Sanh in early 1968 – can only be imagined.

LEFT: Bomb craters pit the ground around a road junction in North Vietnam.

RIGHT: Bridges near Seoul, South Korea, hit by US aircraft during the Communist occupation of the city, early 1951. Destruction on this scale, using ordinary 'iron' bombs, was not easy.

BELOW LEFT: B-52 Stratofortress bombers unload their cargoes over a battlefield target during an 'Arc Light' strike in Vietnam, 1965. The big bombers were restricted to battlefield attacks.

BELOW: B-52s deliver their bombs over a target close to Bien Hoa, South Vietnam, December 1966.

But this was not the only display of US airpower. Since early 1965 President Lyndon B Johnson had been using essentially tactical aircraft such as the McDonnell Douglas F-4 Phantom, North American F-100 Super Sabre and Republic F-105 Thunderchief, to hit selected targets in North Vietnam, under the codename Rolling Thunder. Designed to discourage the North from supporting aggression in the South, as well as to weaken its ability to do so, the campaign was deliberately restrained, like in Korea, to avoid unnecessary escalation. As a result, the B-52s were not involved and the targets, although gradually extended as the North refused to be intimidated, were carefully chosen to avoid civilian deaths as far as possible. It proved to be an expensive method of waging war and one that, by deliberately preventing the knock-out blow so favored by the theorists, was not strategic bombing in the purest sense.

During the period of the Rolling Thunder operation (March 1965-November 1968), North Vietnamese defenses improved significantly, with the Soviets and Communist Chinese providing surface-to-air missiles (SAMs), antiaircraft guns and fighters such as the Mikoyan/Guryevich MiG-21. By the end of 1966 alone, the Americans had lost 455 aircraft over the North, and those airmen who survived to be captured acted as use-

ful hostages when the Communists came to negotiate an American withdrawal a few years later. At the same time, in spite of the many tons of bombs dropped during Rolling Thunder, grave doubts were raised about the effectiveness of the campaign. Claims that 145,000 North Vietnamese were denied to frontline units by being committed to the defense of their homeland, to say nothing of the estimated 500,000 tied down in repair work after the bombing had taken place, were inconclusive evidence of success. The Tet Offensive of early 1968 in fact showed that enemy lines of communication had not been badly affected, supplies of equipment and ammunition had not been seriously reduced and the politburo in the North had not been deterred from its actions in the South. In 1962 General Maxwell Taylor may have

LEFT: Robert S McNamara, US Secretary of Defense under Presidents Kennedy and Johnson in the 1960s, was an early advocate of bombing North Vietnam, he later came to doubt its value.

BELOW: A thermal power plant at Uong Bi, North Vietnam, hit by aircraft from the carrier USS *Constellation*.

BELOW LEFT: F-105 Thunderchiefs refuel.

assured President John F Kennedy that 'North Vietnam is highly vulnerable to conventional bombing,' but six years later more and more people were beginning to agree with the erstwhile Secretary of Defense, Robert S McNamara, that 'the country was predominantly agricultural and had little industry and a rudimentary transport system,' so was unlikely to be affected by a bombing campaign. For this and other political reasons, President Johnson suspended Rolling Thunder in November 1968.

But the lure of bombing remained, and although little air activity took place over the North immediately after 1968, the option of reusing it as a means of applying pressure was not ignored. In 1972 the North Vietnamese mounted a full-scale invasion of the South and President Richard M Nixon had no hesitation in authorizing a resumption of bombing, although to begin with the B-52s were again kept back, devoting their efforts to further Arc Light strikes (which had never ceased) in support of beleaguered South Vietnamese forces. Thus between May and October 1972, in Operation Linebacker, the same sort of essentially tactical aircraft were released over the North with the declared aims of attacking war-related resources, cutting supply lines to the South and isolating North Vietnam from external assistance. The

last of these aims involved attacking railroads which might bring supplies to the North from China, and ports where Chinese and Soviet ships might unload.

There were, therefore, fewer constraints on targets than in Rolling Thunder and, furthermore, more accurate bombs were available. 'Smart' bombs, either TV or laser-guided, could give pinpoint accuracy, and bridges such as the Paul Doumer outside Hanoi and the Thanh Hoa farther south were easily destroyed. American aircraft also carried more sophisticated electronic countermeasures (ECM) in reponse to improved North Vietnamese SAMs, enabling them to survive in the hostile air environment over the North. The damage inflicted during Linebacker was significant, forcing the North Vietnamese to negotiate an end to hostilities more seriously than had been the case before. That, combined with the defense of the South and the use of US airpower in support, undoubtedly prevented a Communist victory in 1972.

The story did not end there, however, for by December 1972 it was obvious that the North's negotiators were still prevaricating and that a peace settlement was as far away as ever. In response, Nixon decided to increase the pressure, releasing the bombers over the North in a short sharp display of power known unofficially as Linebacker II. For the only time in Vietnam, the B-52s were committed for to the North, carrying out an 11-day campaign that was the closest the Americans came to a strategic operation. The Stratofortresses now appeared over Hanoi and Haiphong, aiming for war-related targets but,

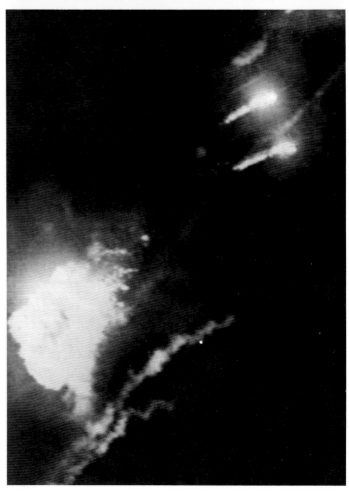

LEFT: A US Navy F-4 Phantom over Vietnam, 1967. Although developed and used as a fighter, the F-4 also proved its worth in Vietnam as an attack bomber, particularly with 'Smart' weapons in 1972.

LEFT: A B-52 explodes over Hanoi after being hit by a SAM-2 missile, Operation Linebacker II, December 1972. The 13-day campaign cost the Americans 15 B-52s.

RIGHT: An F-100 Super Sabre over Vietnam, 1966 – a typical example of the sort of tactical aircraft used by the Americans over the North in Operation Rolling Thunder.

LEFT: B-52s over South Vietnam. The use of such bombers, each capable of delivering over 67,000lbs of ordnance, was devastating during the siege of Khe Sanh in early 1968.

RIGHT: Civilians and members of the local militia inspect the wreckage of a B-52, brought down by SAMs over Hanoi in December 1972. American losses may have seemed high, but the Linebacker II raids did enormous damage.

inevitably, causing civilian casualties. Their exhibition of massive bombing power was designed to persuade the North Vietnamese to return to the conference table and, to a large extent, it seemed to work. Between 18 and 30 December (with a 'pause' over Christmas), the B-52s, backed by fighter-bombers, flew 729 sorties, destroying key features of the Communist war machine – principally oil plants, hydro-electric power stations and air defense systems – which persuaded the politburo in the North that a continuation of hostilities was not in their best interests. The costs were relatively high – the Americans lost 26 aircraft, including 15 B-52s – but in January 1973 a peace settlement was finally hammered out.

The fact that the North Vietnamese signed this agreement and then, within three years, went on to attack the South again, taking over in April 1975, implies that the impact of Linebacker II was only temporary, and for this reason it would be wrong to conclude that strategic bombing had achieved decisive results. However, as a display of American power, it was awesome, suggesting that the heavy bomber, equipped with conventional weapons, still had a role to play, albeit a fairly restricted

one in limited war. A strategic bombing campaign in the traditional sense may have been absent from both the Korean and Vietnam conflicts, but it is interesting to see that the idea still persisted.

This has been shown by a continued pursuit of the 'ideal' bomber, capable of carrying out conventional strategic bombing as well as nuclear strikes in the event of a future war in which restrictions would be lifted. This was particularly apparent in the United States where, in the mid-1970s, the Rockwell B-1 was born. Its backers claimed that by then each B-52 was costing the equivalent of £20,000 per hour of operational flying in terms of fuel and oil alone, and required seven or eight hours' maintenance after each mission. At the equivalent of £62 million a piece, the B-1, capable of carrying nuclear or conventional bombs across the globe and of hitting a small target more accurately than existing missiles, seemed to be a relative bargain. The lowest altitude for modified B-52s was 400 feet; the B-1 would travel at a speed of 700mph at 200 feet. With a top speed of 1350mph at high altitude, this 'strategic super-bomber' would, it was argued, be a war winner. The USAF wanted 244 B-1s to replace its fleet of aging B-52s; a persuasive

additional argument was that the Soviets were placing great faith in the Tupolev Tu-26 Backfire bomber, with a range of 5000 miles, a speed twice that of sound and an ability to deliver missiles 180 miles from its target.

Subsequently canceled for political reasons by President Jimmy Carter in the late-1970s, the B-1 project was resurrected in the form of the B-1B under his successor Ronald Reagan. With a maximum speed of 1451mph at 50,000 feet, the B-1B would fly at 750mph at 500 feet. It would have a range of 6100 miles and a ceiling of 60,000 feet; with a capacity to carry a variety of bomb-loads, it could take 75,000lbs of free-fall conventional bombs internally, plus another 40,000lbs externally. There remained a suspicion, though, that it might not be able to penetrate enemy defenses as easily as its supporters claimed, at least not without missiles blasting a corridor to the target for it. Its main worth might, therefore, be as a platform for stand-off weapons such as the Air-Launched Cruise Missile (ALCM).

The newly developed B-2 ought to overcome these supposed drawbacks. Making use of 'Stealth' technology, the latest American bomber will be able to penetrate known enemy defenses at 600mph at an altitude of 200 feet. Accuracy of bombing, the ability to hit precision targets, would thus be made more certain, and there would be no need to eliminate SAM defenses in advance. In short, the bomber will always get through.

Cautious commentators might well look back to similar claims for the B-17, B-29 and B-52. Only the foolhardy would now suggest that conventional strategic bombing would win a war, even with the B-2. But there is an argument that the strategic bomber, using conventional rather than nuclear bombs, is an essential weapon in the armory of any major power. Its use provides another rung on the ladder of escalation short of the nuclear option. In that sense, the limited use of strategic bombers in Korea and Vietnam suggests that they still have a future. But this can never be to provide a knock-out blow, to destroy civilian morale or to undermine an enemy's industrial capacity to wage war in the way that the theorists had suggested. Douhet once wrote: 'It is always dangerous to keep looking backward when marching forward.' Modern planners would do well to ignore that advice; in the context of conventional strategic bombing, the experience of airmen since 1914 should not be discounted.

ABOVE: A Rockwell B-1B supersonic bomber of the USAF, designed to replace the rather aging fleet of B-52s as part of the American nuclear deterrent 'triad' of land-based missiles, sea-launched missiles and bombers.

RIGHT: A vision of the future – the so-called 'Stealth' bomber, built to be invisible to existing radar. There are doubts being expressed about its effectiveness.

ACKNOWLEDGMENTS

The author and publishers would like to thank Ron Callow for designing this book, Mandy Little for the picture research and Pat Coward for compiling the index. The following agencies and individuals provided photographic material:

Austin J Brown Aviation Picture Library, pages: 67, 78 (bottom).
Brompton Archive, pages: 20-21, 22 (bottom 2), 23 (both), 30 (top), 35 (below), 40 (right), 41 (below), 42 (top), 48, 50-51, 52, 54, 55 (both), 56, 58 (both), 60 (top right), 62 (bottom 2), 66, 75, 78 (top).
Bundesarchiv, pages: 20 (top), 25 (below), 34 (both), 39 (left).
Hulton-Deutsch Collection, pages: 6-7, 15, 31 (top), 36-37, 40 (left), 59 (below), 64-65, 68 (top), 72 (below).
Imperial War Museum, pages: 10 (all 3), 11 (below), 13 (both), 14 (both), 17 (top), 24 (top), 25 (top), 28 (top), 29 (below), 39 (right), 42 (below), 43, 45 (top), 47 (below), 57, 59 (top), 60 (top left), 61 (top left).
Robert Hunt Library, pages: 2-3, 8, 9 (both), 11 (top), 12 (all 3), 16, 18, 19 (both), 24 (below), 26, 27, 28 (below), 29 (top), 30 (below), 32, 33, 35 (top), 38 (both), 44 (top), 46, 47 (top), 49 (both), 63, 69 (below), 70 (below), 71 (both).
Topham Picture Library, pages: 74 (below), 76, 77.
The Research House, pages: US Department of Defense: 70 (top), US Navy: 1, 53, 73, 74 (top).
UPI/Bettmann Newsphotos, pages: 68 (below), 72 (top).
US Air Force, pages: 4-5, 17 (below), 41 (top), 44 (below), 45 (bottom 2), 60 (below), 61 (top right and below), 62 (top).
US Department of Defense, page: 69 (top).